PLAY BALL

The New Baseball Basics for Youth Coaches, Parents, and Kids

Coop DeRenne, Ed.D.
University of Hawaii
California Angels
Pro-Performance, Inc.

Tom House, Ed.D.
Texas Rangers
Bio-Kinetics, Inc.

with

Thomas W. Harris, M.D.
Orthopedic Surgery
Athletic Orthopedic Institute
Elite Athletic Performance Consultant,
Texas Rangers

Barton Buxton, Ed. D., A.T.C.
University of Hawaii

West Publishing Company
Minneapolis/St. Paul   New York   Los Angeles   San Francisco

WEST'S COMMITMENT TO THE ENVIRONMENT

In 1906, West Publishing Company began recycling materials left over from the production of books. This began a tradition of efficient and responsible use of resources. Today, up to 95% of our legal books and 70% of our college and school texts are printed on recycled, acid-free stock. West also recycles nearly 22 million pounds of scrap paper annually—the equivalent of 181,717 trees. Since the 1960s, West has devised ways to capture and recycle waste inks, solvents, oils, and vapors created in the printing process. We also recycle plastics of all kinds, wood, glass, corrugated cardboard, and batteries, and have eliminated the use of styrofoam book packaging. We at West are proud of the longevity and the scope of our commitment to the environment.

Prepress, Printing and Binding by West Publishing Company.

 PRINTED ON 10% POST CONSUMER RECYCLED PAPER

A West Custom Publication
COPYRIGHT ©1993 by WEST PUBLISHING COMPANY
610 Opperman Drive
P.O. Box 64526
St. Paul, MN 55164-0526

00 99 98 97 96 95 94 93   8 7 6 5 4 3 2 1 0

ISBN 0-314-02575-8

DEDICATION

This coaching-parent text is dedicated to my son, Keoni DeRenne, 14, his youth sports coaches and our International Baptist Church's leadership staff. Thank you all for your positive influences that have helped contribute to the development of Keoni's athletic abilities and his Christian character. Good luck youth coaches; you have an awesome task!

CONTENTS

ABOUT THE AUTHORS

Dr. Coop DeRenne has been an Exercise and Sport Scientist at the University of Hawaii-Manoa for the past seventeen years. During this time he has pioneered a new supplemental weight training field he coined, "Weighted Implement Training." He leads the country in baseball research; and specifically, he supervised sixteen hitting and pitching warm-up, exercise, biomechanical, and visual research projects using over 600 amateur and professional hitters and pitchers as his "laboratory" subjects.

During the past 37 years, Coop has participated and coached in youth amateur leagues, high schools, at the university level, and in professional baseball. He has been a major league research consultant, professional player, minor league instructor, and is currently the research consultant to Ray Poitevint, Vice-President, International Operations, California Angels. He has a unique baseball background combining science with hands-on-field experience.

Coop has authored two other books with West Publishing Company; *Power Baseball* with Tom House, and *High-Tech Hitting: Science vs. Tradition.*

Tom House has enjoyed a successful baseball career. He was an All-American pitcher at the University of Southern California and a high draft choice by the Atlanta Braves. He pitched in the big leagues for eight years and then became a minor league pitching coach with the San Diego Padres. He has been a major league pitching coach for the Texas Rangers the last seven years.

House has written and produced more pitching books and instructional videotapes than anyone in the history of the game. He has university and advanced degrees in marketing, nutrition, and sports psychology. He also has a unique background combining science with hands-on-field experience.

Dr. Tom Harris is one of the leading sports medicine orthopedics in the country. He is the founder and director of The Athletic Orthopedic Institute in San Diego, California. He is the physician for the U.S.A. National Ski Team, and one of the Texas Rangers' orthopedic physicians.

Dr. Barton Buxton is an assistant professor at the University of Hawaii-Manoa. He has a joint appointment in the Department of Health, Physical Education and Recreation (HPER) and the John A. Burns School of Medicine. He is also the Athletic Training Education Program Director in HPER. Dr. Buxton is the sports medicine consultant for Hawaii Youth Sports and Fitness Program and a reviewer for the *Journal of Sports Rehabilitation*.

INTRODUCTION

We commend and applaud all the parents and parent-coaches of our youth baseball leagues around the country. Your love and dedication for your children and baseball is unmeasurable. You have chosen baseball (the sports world) as a vehicle to help you with the most difficult task on earth---the raising of your child. This is an awesome responsibility. We hope the information presented will lighten the load, help give you more peace of mind, give enjoyment to you and your child, and help foster an everlasting friendship between all the members of your family.

Research surveys show that the major force behind the rehabilitating of young delinquents or despondent children is the impact of sports. Organized sports is part of the humanitarian crusade to save our children from the "evils" of our society. Sports changes lives, gives direction to lost "souls" and provides a wholesome family environment.

You are an integral and vital part of this crusade. You may never know or see the impact you directly have on the lives of our children, but believe us, we have seen this impact. Thank you for caring and reaching out!

Let us help you...Because of your job and other family commitments, we realize your time is limited as you individually work with your child's baseball skills and/or when you spend time coaching your youth team. As baseball and sports medicine professionals, we have an advantage---baseball is our life. Therefore, let us bring information and practical application to you, and in so doing, help you become better equipped to coach and teach your child and team.

The information presented is not based on theories or opinions. Our information is research-proven. This is our commitment to the baseball communities. We will only provide you with the latest and best information. We also have youth baseball children of our own, which motivates us to provide them and their respective coaches with research-proven information. We want to see our children develop to their maximum genetic potentials. Again, we hope we have been valuable assets for you with your coaching careers, and assisting you as you work with your baseball son or daughter. Good luck!

-- Dr. Coop DeRenne

Section One

THE THREE I's
INFORM, INSTRUCT, INSPIRE

I
Mental Conditioning

"Good intentions are NO replacement for good information."

--Tom House

Parent/coach, no matter how good your intentions are, you must **INFORM, INSTRUCT AND INSPIRE**. These three "I's" are the keys to coaching success. In order to inform, instruct and inspire, you must have good **INFORMATION**. Good intentions are not enough to get the job done. Remember, in spite of your good intentions and in spite of your well-meaning efforts, you can be a detrimental factor to the playing careers of your players.

Our role is to provide you with research-proven and field tested information. We desire to put good information into the hands of well-meaning parents and coaches. We will guide you along this journey.

IMPACT

Coaches, you have an awesome task.   Your behavior and teaching/coaching abilities will have an everlasting impact on young players. This impact may help or hinder the character building process of your players.

The careers of successful coaches have a positive impact on their respective players because they never lose sight of their three most important and measurable objectives:

- **Character building.**
- **Fitness development.**
- **Skill development.**

The desired outcome is not a skilled major league player, but a *responsible and productive citizen*. This outcome is only attainable if we give players a positive growing athletic experience within a warm, friendly, healthy, and safe environment.

Keep in mind the negative flip side is that 75% of all youth sports participants drop out of organized sports by ages 13-14. If we don't do our jobs properly, we will contribute to this drop-out rate. The alternative for these drop-outs is the streets.   And research reveals that more teenagers are dying from bullets than natural causes. Therefore, your impact will lead to either streetwise or citizen-wise characters. Look in the mirror, what are your intentions, what will be your impact on our youth?

SPORTSMANSHIP

Sportsmanship begins with the coach and parents. We cannot be sending "mixed messages" to our players. If we desire good sportsmanship from our teams, then we must be good sports as well. Remember, be a positive role model. Sportsmanship are noticeable behaviors. These behaviors are attitudes put into action. Therefore, coaches, if we want proper sportsmanship behaviors, we must teach and reinforce only acceptable attitudes. *Proper behavior is the by-product of a good attitude.*

Examples of Sportsmanlike Behavior:

- Have a good attitude.
- Being a good winner and loser.
- Respecting the officials' decisions.
- Playing by the rules.
- Shaking hands after competition.
- Respecting coaches' decisions.
- Avoid unnecessary roughness.
- Helping an opponent up.
- Avoiding verbal exchanges with opponents.
- Respecting your opponent.

Develop a Sportsmanship Code of Conduct with your players.

How good of a coach are you, or how good do you want to be? Your answer for success must be measured against the young athlete's BILL OF RIGHTS!

BILL OF RIGHTS

- Every young athlete has a right to participate in sports.

- Every young athlete has a right to participate at a level commensurate with his maturity and ability.

- Every young athlete has a right to have QUALIFIED adult leadership.

- Every young athlete has a right to PLAY as a child and not as an adult.

- Every young athlete has a right to share in the leadership and decision-making processes.

- Every young athlete has a right to participate in a safe and healthy environment.

- Every young athlete has a right to participate in proper preparation and conditioning.

- Every young athlete has a right for equal opportunity to strive for success.

- Every young athlete has a right to be treated with dignity.

- **MOST IMPORTANT:** Every young athlete has a right to have FUN in sports!

*Most of us have violated one or more of these rights more times than we like to admit. We must never lose sight that we are working with immature children, who do not think as adults, who do not act like adults, and who do not PLAY like adults. Treat your players as children and give them discipline, room to act their age, room to succeed, a sense of responsibility and commitment, time for self-motivation, good information, fun, love and your commitment to be the best coach you can be.

IDEAL ENVIRONMENT

<u>The Absolutes of a Top Performance</u>

THE GOAL OF EVERY COACH IS TO HELP THE ATHLETE IMPLEMENT THE ABSOLUTES THAT ARE REQUIRED TO GET THE MOST OUT OF HIS PHYSICAL PERFORMANCE. These absolutes are as follows:

- Mental Conditioning
- Physical Conditioning
- Nutritional Conditioning
- Visual Conditioning
- Biomechanical Conditioning:
  Mechanics of the Position

Corollary: Coach, find that proper balance to integrate emotional and mental qualities and nutritional aspects with the physical-biomechanical-skill requirements of a particular position based on the individual's performance capabilities.

This *holistic balance* will enhance player performances. The conditioning absolutes are pieces of the athlete's performance puzzle. If any one of those pieces is missing, then the young athlete's potential is retarded.

It is not enough to send your son or daughter off to practice with a candy bar, a pat on the back and expect him or her to return that night a superstar full of learned skills and enjoyment. Because all of us live in the "fast lane," with drive-thru everything, we use the "no time" or on-the-go and rushing excuses to not spend time developing our children's capabilities. It takes time and careful planning to develop the holistic conditioning components within your child's growing body. As a parent/coach, your first responsibility is to aid you child's and team's holistic development during the time you have with them.

GAME PERFORMANCE

Preparing the athlete according to the five conditioning absolutes gives the player a vital foundational edge. But this preparation does not assure the athlete of a top performance. On game day, he must be relaxed, confident and concentrate, or his potential won't be reached.

Relaxation, concentration and confidence are trainable skills. All three skills are a function of preparation. Preparation is a junction of good information and organization.

Ⓑ *COACHING TIP*

> *The bottom line to coaching success is the Three I's: Inform, Instruct and Inspire.*

FEAR

There are three kinds of athletic fear:

- Physical fear of getting hurt.
- Fear of success: how to handle it.
- Fear of failure.

In order for your child and players to reach their genetic potentials, your players must learn, with your help, how to control these fears.

One of the most frustrating things for a dad who has great intentions but poor information is to see his child or one of his players afraid. Before the afraid player can become teachable his fear must be overcome.

EXAMPLE

Dad is throwing batting practice to his fearful son. Pitch after pitch the boy continuously steps "into the bucket" because he is afraid of getting hit by the ball. Dad says, "You are stepping in the bucket, don't be afraid of the ball. It doesn't hurt when it hits you. Come on---it won't hurt you! You're being a wimp. This ball can't hurt you." But, that's not true. The son knows and so does the father that getting hit with the baseball hurts.

Coach, you must get this concept across to the player---it is OK to be afraid. There is nothing wrong with being afraid. It is how you deal with your player's fear that will help him to become a successful or unsuccessful competitor.

EXAMPLE

Joe Niekro was a big league pitcher. Joe smoked. On the day of a game, he was so scared he could not even light his own cigarette. But, he admitted his fear, and still went out trusting his preparation, ability, and became a successful major league pitcher. He learned how to deal with his fear.

Niekro did not let his fear hinder his performances and thirst for competition. The satisfaction that Niekro received from competition and developing his skills outweighed his fears of being hurt, fear of success, and fear of failure.

Fear of Success

How a player handles FEAR OF SUCCESS is important along his learning journey. The more successful a player becomes the more expectations the public and his family have of him. It then can become difficult for the player to meet those higher expectations. Coach, it is up to you to Provide empathetic counsel. **Help him to understand that this fear is normal, and that he will not be a failure if he doesn't meet his or others expectations. He must understand that his fear is self-inflicted.** A positive and realistic attitude can minimize this fear and pressure factor. Coach, work with the performer's attitude.

Fear of Failing

This is a very common performance inhibitor with many amateur and professional athletes.

If you ask a professional player or an amateur high school or collegiate player "head-to-head," if they are afraid to fail, none of them are. Pitchers realize they can't get every hitter out, and hitters know they can't get a hit every time up. No one can succeed every time he goes out to compete. And, his team can't win every ball game.

The young players do not understand that it is not the fear of failing, but **IT IS THE FEAR OF THE FEELING OF FAILING** that they have difficulty coping with. Coach, this is where you have to help the young athlete understand the difference. We are not afraid to fail or lose. What we are at odds with is the feeling that goes with failure. Understand, **YOU MUST FAIL TO LEARN. YOU MUST FAIL TO GET FEEDBACK IN ORDER TO GET BETTER.**

But unfortunately, feelings come not only with successes, but with failures. It is how young players cope with those psycho-emotional feelings that determine more often than not the successful competitor. As an instructor, as a parent, and as a coach, you can help the player understand the feelings of failure are just that---feelings. If you only assess them as a point in time, then they will only last temporarily. **FAILING DOESN'T MAKE YOU A FAILURE UNLESS YOU GIVE INTO FAILING.**

If you "throw in the towel" and say, "I can't" or "I won't," and if you let the negative thoughts get away from you, then you have in effect become a failure. Then you have every right to fear those specific feelings.

PAIN VS. STIFFNESS

"Come on---you can gut it out. Tough it out. Don't be a wimp. Get out of here---go play. Grow up and be a MAN!" We all have said these negative statements at one time or another. How do you know the player's pain really isn't serious, or is it stiffness in disguise?

Coach, PAIN vs. STIFFNESS is a difficult concept to understand for a 12-13 year old who is trying on his manhood or her womanhood and doesn't want to give into pain at the expense of performance. He really doesn't know how to assess what is HURT and what is just STIFFNESS.

Stiffness goes away when you loosen-up to warm-up to do your activity. On practice day or game day the sequence is always the same: you loosen-up to warm-up to do your particular activity for the day. Stiffness will go away in your loosening up and warming up phases during your practice or competitive day.

Pain, on the other hand, no matter what you do in the loosening up or warming up process, will not go away. No matter, if it is a sharp burning pain, or a deep constant pain, in your loosening up and warming up phases, the pain does not go away. A young player should never be made to perform if he is in pain. He will run the risk of long-term injury, and he will not be able to perform up to his practice and competitive capabilities. It is only a dead-end.

Coach, you must teach your players to learn to listen to their bodies. You, in return should be sensitive to your players' feelings and complaints. THE BODY IS NOT DUMB IF YOU LET IT BE SMART!

TOLERANCE

Every athlete's primary purpose on any given day, in practices or in games, is to take himself to the edge of TOLERANCE. You never want to go beyond.   NO PAIN, NO GAIN, is NOT a good approach to maximizing performance. If you push through pain to gain, you never will be as good as you could be if you approached gain by taking WORK to tolerance. Approach gain every day by committing yourself to being the best you can be mentally, physically, and psycho-emotionally. Take everything you can under control to tolerance.   If you do that, in the weight room, on the practice field, and in the competitive environment (if you "never get over your skis") then the human body and mind will adapt to the new stress and tolerance levels. Gradually and systematically as you move just beyond your tolerance level, the body will get stronger and perform better until you "max" out at your genetic capability.

EXAMPLE

The over-achiever, the player that seems to get more out of his ability than what his ability would dictate, is the person that matches up the MENTAL, PHYSICAL, AND BIO-MECHANICS OF HIS SKILL with maximizing to tolerance. He will always perform one notch above his limited mental, or physical or biomechanical limitations. This is called SYNERGY. Synergy with athletic performance means that the whole of the performance is greater than the sum of its parts. This is the ultimate compliment for an athlete and coach. They can say, "I am a better athlete or coach today than yesterday. I am competing with all cylinders 'maxed' out."

Take everything to tolerance. Don't ask more out of a young athlete than he is capable of giving. But ask him to give whatever his body, mind, and emotions will tolerate. That strength will come in all the above aspects with continuous positive reinforcement and actual experience of competition.

FORMULAS FOR PRACTICAL APPLICATION

Formula 1:

Information + Experience = Knowledge

What is knowledge?
Coach, who are you?

- *The Unconscious-Incompetent Coach.* He knows not what he knows not. This parent-coach is basically a fool and is causing a lot of difficulties for the athletes he is working with.

- *The Conscious-Incompetent Coach.* He know not, and knows that he knows not. He is ignorant, but he is teachable. Dad and Mom, this book is written for you.

- *The Unconscious-Competent Coach.* He knows and knows not that he knows. This is the dad or mom who is basically asleep. WAKE-UP!! You have a lot more information in your brain than you are aware of, but you are not utilizing your good information properly.

- *The Conscious-Competent Coach.* He knows and he knows that he knows. You are WISE! You have the information and the experience and therefore, YOU HAVE THE KNOWLEDGE. Our goal for you is to make you better!

Formula 2:

With Knowledge Comes AWARENESS...

Awareness of what can go RIGHT and
Awareness of what can go WRONG.

If you have good information, practical experience, and have gained some knowledge, you are dwelling more on what can go right and less on what can go wrong! This is a positive outlook. Find the "positive" in every situation. Dwell on what works, not what doesn't work. From pitch to pitch on the field, and in our everyday living, we have to ADJUST. This adjustment comes from being aware of rights or wrongs, and adjusting accordingly. When you are positive and seeking to find out what works best for you and your players, you are stimulating growth and fostering healthy attitudes. If the attitude is right within your team, then they are ready to learn. You have created the ideal learning environment.

Negative motivation works only in the SHORT-TERM. If you deal with positive thinking, positive reinforcement and visualization---focusing on what can go right a lot more than on what can go wrong---the young athlete in the long-term will be aware that you want him to feel good about himself and want him to succeed. Likewise, as you disseminate your information and coaching techniques in the positive light, you will be received more affirmatively and have more of a chance for a character-shaping impact!

INNER MAKEUP

Coaches have a tremendous impact on the characters' of their players. If you want to be a positive force, to influence your players to make the right decisions and head them in the right direction, you first must strengthen your inner-self. **One's character or makeup guides his life.** Look inside, are you all that you want to be? Are stable, prepared to learn and instruct, dedicated, communicative, loving and giving? Ask your players, they will tell you. You can't hide anything from your players.

Your coaching philosophy and style is a reflection of your inner strengths and makeup. You want positive results with your players, then look at yourself for direction. Molding and shaping the lives of our youth is an awesome task.

Therefore, you don't need any excess character flaws---shouting, foul language, demeaning verbiage, etc.

How do you strengthen your inner-self? First, practice good moral behavior---**be a good role model**. Second, your work ethics must be skillfully planned and consistent. Third, build your character upon a solid foundation of information. It is not enough to have good intentions, or to be a giving coach, you must be a knowledgeable and morally good role model. Remember, good coaching is three-fold:

- INFORMING
- INSTRUCTING   > **THROUGH POSITIVE CONDUCT**
- INSPIRING

⑪ *COACHING TIP*

> *Coach, you wear your values. What you think, what you feel and what you show, is yourself. Put on integrity and class.*

Now you are ready to mold and influence your players' characters. HOW?

You need to find out how kids learn. How to motivate them. How to communicate with them on their level. Learn how to treat these young players as you would want them to treat you. In all that you do, be CONSISTENT, LOVING, GIVING, RESPECTFUL, INSPIRING AND KNOWLEDGEABLE.

To help you along this character-shaping journey, you need to understand some basic inner quality terminology.

ATHLETIC POTENTIAL

Athletic potential is a function of natural ability co-existing with learned training and technique development, working in tandem with an inner desire. Coach, you must utilize the athlete's natural ability to help you develop his sport-skills throughout proper training and motivation, which will result in a holistic effort that will enable your player to get the most out of himself. This is your goal---to maximize the athletic potential in every one of your players.

ATTITUDE

There are releasing mechanisms that allow your mind to get into alignment with what you can do for the player. This is a function of **AWARENESS**. You must have an open mind. You should be willing to accept change. You have to be willing to review and repeat. All of you have some objective or goal to direct your conscious, your subconscious, your physical, and your emotional efforts towards positive production. The practical component of these releasing mechanisms is called **ATTITUDE**. Attitudes are habits of thinking and directions in which we lean. Shaping the players' attitudes is a three-dimensional process:

- It comes in words.
- It comes in visualized pictures or images.
- It comes in feelings.

On and off the field use these three mediums to convey your feelings as you are forming the positive attitudes within your players.

You must understand that young players' habits, their thought processes, and their emotional responses to the athletic environment will help you to formulate your own attitudes and understand the desires of your players. Also the way we track these attitudinal mechanisms---coach to athlete and athlete to coach---will also help you determine the direction to lean not only in the short-term on a day-to-day basis with practices and games, but with your medium and long-term seasonal goals.

EXAMPLE

Why do so many little leaguers quit the game after 12-15? The reason so many little leaguers who have talent and potential burnout and don't perform in high school is because their motivation, learning potential, and attitudes have all been skewed in a negative direction.

Attitude = Personal Choices + Behavioral Commitment

Attitudes are behavioral clothes.

LEARNING

Learning is gaining positive information from successful outcomes. Learning is coping with failing, and at the same time understanding that if you fail, you are not a failure.

One quality of any successful individual is that he understands that failing does not make him a failure. In fact, successful individuals, more often than not, will fail more often than unsuccessful people because it shows their willingness to take a chance. Coach, point this out to your players. If they learn from their failures, they can succeed next time. Explain to your players that the only way for them to know how good they can be in areas where they have never experienced is to try them! Succeed and fail with them and you both will learn from those SUCCESSES and FAILURES.

Therefore, your goal is to put into a young athlete's physical and mental makeup an image that **HE CAN AND HE WILL, IF HE DOES.** If you can sustain this idea when dealing with your players, then you have INFORMED, INSTRUCTED AND INSPIRED. Each player will believe HE IS, HE CAN, and HE WILL!

Fuel

What fuels this composite of successful, motivational and informational processing that goes on in the young athlete's mind is LEARNING. When learning is required, the interface between athlete and coach must take place efficiently (relationship of work and energy), effectively (appropriate information for successful movement) with feedback.

Otherwise, striving to achieve athletic performance is halted and both player and coach will "suboptimize"---achieve less than they are both capable of doing.

Learning takes place through direct communication through the five senses. The communication process must be reciprocated back and forth because seldom is there a time when the athlete's needs and the coach's needs are realized simultaneously by player and coach. **If the coach realized the player's need first, he must in effect: INFORM, INSTRUCT AND INSPIRE!**

Usually, the coach will realize the player's need way before the player will. Coach, you will have to "hold his hand" through the learning process.

One of the results of learning is CONFIDENCE. If a player feels confident his chance of a better performance increases. Confidence in return enhances self-esteem.

In summary, what is the learning process? SEE IT, FEEL IT, DO IT!

Learning Components

Learning by definition helps to determine appropriate behavior that will match-up motivation with physical activity.

There are three components to learning: (1) learning processes, (2) learning methods, and (3) learning outcomes---the results which lead to an injury free athletic performance in a competitive environment.

- Learning processes: Learning comes through sensory mechanisms, perceptual mechanisms, conceptual mechanisms, perceptual-motor (visual) and memory recall.

- Learning methods: trial and error, imitation, feedback conditioning from skill learning (stimulus-response-reward-feedback) and cognitive reasoning.   Our experience supports the imitation method (neuromuscular memory) as the best and quickest way a young athlete learns.

EXAMPLE

Use your best skill player to demonstrate.   The less talented but inspired players will try to emulate that athlete.

EXAMPLE

Cognition Methodology: Coach, try to eliminate dissonance in a young athlete's mind.   As a coach, if you give him conflicting messages, double standards, or beliefs that negate each other, you will cause disharmony in his thought processes.   As the young athlete is gathering information and getting instruction, and as he is showing self-discipline as he works, if you are sending him "mixed messages" (conflicting beliefs) he will have dissonance in his mind.   Dissonance will reduce his ability to compete.

Therefore, you must give accurate and positive information, be a consistent role model ("WEAR YOUR BELIEFS") and make consistent decisions that will be supportive not conflicting.

* Learning Outcomes: If all has gone well from learning, the outcomes from learning will be: (1) facts that make sense, (2) improved physical skills, (3) acquired attitudes that support both the facts and skills, and (4) acquired positive behavior patterns that will "carry" an athlete when he is in a "foreign situation" or in an adrenalin rush (tight situation) through the negative into a positive experiential competitive outcome.

⑪ *COACHING TIP*

All the composite information above will contribute to your knowledge base, the development of your reasoning, and enhance your ability to make mental and physical decisions in the competitive environment.

HOUSE'S INTERPRETATION

Difference Between Winners and Losers

Coach, you must understand the following differences between winners and losers.

- **Winners see what they want** and losers see what they want to avoid!

- **Winners dwell on past successes and wins,** losers dwell on past failures or losses.

Players and coaches, be winners. See what you want---center on the positive and make it be real. Dwell on what you have done in the past that has been successful. And those past successful experiences will help you reinforce in an affirmative way where you want to be today.

House's Laws for Success

SUCCESS is a function of PREPARATION meeting OPPORTUNITY. OPPORTUNITY will always come disguised as HARD WORK. WORK is something that the body does not want to do. MOTIVATION is something that the mind does to convince the body to WORK. Therefore, all PREPARATION is PLANNED MOTIVATION.

Plan your work, and work your plan. Be organized. Plan every practice very carefully. As you plan the basic rudiments of practices and games, also plan your motivational strategies and techniques. Good communication is not only what you say, but HOW YOU SAY IT.

SUCCESS also is your interpretation of yourself-esteem. The five components of self-esteemed success are as follows: (1) enjoyable experiences, (2) experiences that were fulfilling, (3) accomplishments, (4) your own interpretation of your best self and not others' opinions of what they think of you, and (5) recognizing you are steadily moving positively toward worthwhile predetermined goals that match up with your potential.

Coach, success with your athletes is more of a JOURNEY than a destination. It is very important that you understand that this journey leads automatically to winning and losing. **But until a player makes his living in professional athletics, winning and losing should not be the goal of athletic competition.**

Another tool you can use to promote a positive successful behavior in your players is to focus on what can go RIGHT more than what can go wrong within the competitive environment. Remember, your coaching prospective will be different than from your on-field player's point of view. Therefore, you need to have a "meeting of the minds." Your players need to know explicitly what you are thinking and what is expected of them in every situation. Also, you need to know what your players are thinking so you can make the necessary adjustments.

There must be harmony between the coach and his players. If harmony exists, you have increased the team's chances for success. Once you have fostered this harmony, then focus on all the things that can go right in every situation, thereby teaching the players how to adjust positively under pressure. The better they handle pressure, the more chance they will have for success.

Remember, success is measured, not in terms of winning, but in providing your players with the necessary motivation, information and opportunity in a planned environment for each one to taste some degree of success. In other words, **put every player in a planned situation so that they all can succeed.**

Therefore, as a coach, you must synthesize all this new information and put everything in the correct perspective to enhance the player's skills as you provide him with an enjoyable and meaningful learning environment.

Please remember, don't put "the cart before the horse" by emphasizing winning or losing. Let winning and losing happen as a byproduct within the teaching-learning environment.

⓪ *COACHING TIP*

Research points out that one hour after a game, 65-70% of little leaguers can't remember the score of the game, and most of them don't even care who won or lost. But, after the game, they will recall having a good time or a bad time while they are competing. To the young athlete success is not measured in wins or losses, but how he played the game---was it fun and did he do something positive to make himself feel good?

Affirmations

AFFIRMATIONS are positive statements or thoughts. These positive statements are tools in the communication process between coach and player. The affirmation contains instructional information transferred by coaches to players in order to enhance skill development and improve players' self-esteem. Areas of information include: (1) physical conditioning, (2) nutritional conditioning, (3) biomechanical conditioning, (4) visual conditioning, and (5) mental conditioning.

In many cases, most athletes are not willingly doing the things required by them to get the most out of their abilities. Work is not fun. Unless you become creative and disguise the work elements of practice as fun activities, you will always struggle with some of your players. Not many young players are intrinsically motivated to work. Affirmations are good psychological tools and should be used in tandem with fun practices.

If you reinforce with consistent affirmations the required positive behavior you so desire within your players, you will see negative

behaviors change. Remember, back your praise with actions---show you care and earnestly want to help your players grow.

Coach, it is important to understand that if you are not using affirmations, you are probably criticizing and indirectly encouraging negative behaviors. Criticism turns young players off. If your boss criticized your performance at work, your reactionary behavior would be negative. This behavior will result in a delaying of your motivation to solve the problem. Young players are no different. That is why a player can't make an instant adjustment to the next pitch while at bat once his coach has yelled at him. The distraught young player now loses his concentration of the task at hand because of the fear of failure his coach has instilled in him. No one can compete if they are scared.

If you criticize a young player, you are attacking his self-esteem. You may lose the player's respect for you forever, or at least the two-way communication process is probably stopped. Now, because of his negative feelings toward you and his fear of failure, his journey toward a more positive behavior and skill developmental progress will be impeded.

It is very important to listen to your player's suggestions and evaluation. If you only listen to yourself, you will have a tendency not to hear or see. It is easy to blame the young player. But, most of the time the blame should rest on your shoulders.

EXAMPLE

"You folks enjoyed this workout. You are doing it because you want to do it everyday. We are having fun while we work. I can see you enjoyed taking lots of ground balls. You all are good listeners. You are doing a great job doing the things that I am asking you to do in this practice." Talking to the group (singling out one player), "I enjoyed our discussion today, your ideas are super! We are going to work on this as a group, and thanks for your contribution."

Coach, every time you communicate with a young player relate to him on the plus side not the negative side. Use positive communication as you inform, instruct, and inspire. Behavioral changes will occur through a good communication process.

As you become more of a positive communicator through the use of daily affirmations while displaying a consistent exemplary behavior, your coaching ability will dramatically improve. Remember, your coaching career is a journey toward self-improvement and player development.

ⓐ *COACHING TIP*

PRAISE IN PUBLIC AND CRITICIZE IN PRIVATE.

Psychological Vitamins

Sports psychologists inhale and regurgitate psychological vitamins. These are phrases or words that feed a youngster's ego, feed his self-confidence and feed his self-worth. Coach, you must follow these leaders, and start popping your own affirmable vitamins: "Thank you," "Good boy," "That a boy," "That's right," "Let's play," "I'll be glad to do it with you," "Sure I'll watch," "You're so smart," "Isn't this good," "Isn't this fun," "Hey, you are really something special."

The directions on the "psychological vitamins" bottle you purchased should read:

- Give approval.
- Give praise.
- Give recognition.
- Give affection.
- Smile a lot.
- Accept the player as he is.

- Display positive body language.
- Place a player in a selective situation that will increase his chances of succeeding.

Toxins or Anti-Vitamins include:

- Words of disapproval, failure, criticism, hostility, and rejection.
- Being ignored.
- Negative body language---frowning, pointing of finger, shaking of head, tightening of clenched fists, slapping hands together in disgust, etc.
- Phrases to avoid: "No, how many times...," "Stop it," "Shut up," "Sit on it," "I won't care if you like it or you don't."

Coach, research tells us that as you are analyzing your completed practice or game, if your athletes were emotionally stable and physically productive, chances are you gave them THREE times the amount of psychological vitamins as compared to the negative toxins.

⑪ *COACHING TIP*

When evaluating, be analytical not emotional. In the "heat" of battle, be cool. Don't exhale verbal toxins. They are deadly and attack self-esteem.

BURNOUT

We take the risk of athletic burnout by starting our children's competitive nature at an early age with organized sports. All too often a child prodigy quits too soon because of "pushy" parents, overzealous coaches, and a year round commitment to a single sport. To avoid burnout, follow these suggestions:

- Participate in multiple activities.
- Parents, don't push, but guide and direct.
- Emphasize FUN and EFFORT, not winning.

Box Score

At the end of each week, read House's poem. This thought is the culmination of this chapter.

Just a Little Boy

He stands at the plate with heart pounding fast,
the bases are loading, the die has been cast,
Mom and dad can't help him--he stands alone,
A hit at this moment would send the team home,
The ball reaches the plate--he swings and he misses,
There is a groan from the crowd with some boos and some hisses,
A thoughtless voice cries, strikeout the bum,
Tears fill his eyes--the game is no longer fun...
So open your heart and give him a break,
For it's moments like this
That a MAN you can make.
Keep this in mind, when you hear someone forget,
He's just a little boy, and not a man yet.

●●●●●●●●●●●●

When you are INFORMING, INSTRUCTING, and INSPIRING, remember, *do not* expect your young players to perform like adults. They should not have to carry any pain--be it mental, physical, or psycho-emotional to practices or games. DON'T ASK MORE OUT OF AN ATHLETE THAN WHAT HE CAN GIVE YOU!

At the youthful age, *let them be kids.* FUN FIRST, then information, then instruction, then inspiration. Let winning and losing happen.

EXAMPLE

Visualize This Scenario

A little boy walks through the front door and says to Mommy, "Mommy, you don't have to hug me this time, we won."

II
Practice and Game
Preparation

*"If you fail to plan,
  you're planning to fail."*

--Dr. Coop DeRenne

When planning your practices and games, you must plan the daily sessions with the player's Bill of Rights in mind.

Coach, you must understand that the underlying philosophy of planning is to remember: **"BASEBALL IS A TEAM SPORT MADE-UP OF INDIVIDUALS."** In youth baseball, the team is composed of individual KIDS. No way can you treat them like adults and expect them to play error-free like adults. These young players are children with their own immature behaviors.   Treat them as individuals with team rules for discipline and unity.   BUT, YOU MUST COMMUNICATE WITH THEM INDIVIDUALLY AND LOVE THEM EQUALLY.

PROBLEM IDENTIFICATION IS HALF THE SOLUTION. Coach, first look within yourself for the problem, then at your players. Maybe you are the cause! Find the solution through good information, then instruct and inspire.

LESS TALK, MORE ACTION---Children learn more by doing than by listening to your instruction. Do not spend a lot of time explaining how (new skills); demonstrate, then let them experiment and experience. Allow the neuromuscular memory process to become effective.

Players learn by doing more repetitions and then more repetitions. Practices should be well thought out as to produce as many skill repetitions as possible within the normal time constraints of practice. This idea reinforces the neuromuscular memory theory. Practices should not take longer than two hours.   Therefore, do not waste valuable time. **HUSTLE IS NOT OPTIONAL, IT IS MANDATORY. No one ever walks on the baseball field, including the coaches.**

PLAN OF ACTION

The coach should formulate a set of goals that he hopes to achieve. These goals should be obtained by informing, instructing, and inspiring his players. Though, goals are long-term or seasonal, they will be acquired little by little by the young players in daily practices. Therefore, coach, you must in daily practices create specific player objectives, in order for your seasonal outcomes to be attained.

For yourself and for your players, create exciting and imaginative goals and objectives centered on the following themes:

- Player behavioral and skill developments.
- Proper player work ethic and conduct.
- Improve player game performances and competitive behaviors.

You must continually re-evaluate and restate objectives and goals in PRESENT TENSE AFFIRMATIONS. You want to affirm what you are after, all the time.

EXAMPLES---SEASONAL GOALS

- The players will obtain the acceptable behavior: self-discipline, self-motivation, good sportsmanship, and to become COACHABLE AND TEACHABLE.
- The players will learn and understand the basic rudiments of their skill position.
- The players will learn how to approach a competitive game so as to attain maximum out of their mental and physical talents.
- The players will have fun during the learning and competitive environments.
- The players will learn that winning and losing are secondary.

How do we create these objectives and goals? How do we select the right strategies to obtain player objectives and goals?...

The behavioral formula that will help you to define your individualized and specific player objectives and goals, and at the same time help you select the proper strategies to direct your efforts is simply:

**ACTUAL BEHAVIOR + DESIRED BEHAVIOR =
COACHABLE CONDUCT**

There is nothing more important than developing the character of a player. Direct the player to the acceptable behavior. As he improves his conduct, he will become more attentive and coachable. **Once he becomes, "COACHABLE," he is TEACHABLE.**

How do you change his behavior to the acceptable conduct so he can become coachable? **ACCEPT THE PLAYER FOR WHO HE IS and INFORM, INSTRUCT and INSPIRE.**

HANDS ON:
See It, Feel It, Do It

To produce the right behavior within your players, you must further understand how they learn. As they become coachable and teachable, your players' characters will change to the acceptable behaviors. As their behaviors change, you will see improvements in their skill development.

Learning also comes through the five senses. When you use your eyes to read or witness something new, learning takes place. When you meditate and develop an understanding of what you have learned and put it into practical application, then it is said that you come to a point that YOU KNOW. This is the Cognitive Domain.

Learning can also take place through the Affective Domain. This is your sensory mechanism in your body---your feelings. When the body is touched or feels, learning is taking place.

As the body moves, it is aware either consciously or subconsciously of where it is and how it is moving through space. This body awareness is called KINESTHETIC or PROPRIOCEPTION AWARENESS. Kinesthetic (Psycho-Motor Domain) awareness is another form of learning. The body learns by doing. As you know, some athletes learn a new physical skill much more easily, more quickly and more efficiently than others. The more kinesthetic awareness the athlete has, the more he learns and the better he moves or performs. Because of his superior kinesthetic awareness, the superior athlete also has better instincts and better game sense than the average player.

Coach, athletes in general will learn more readily and efficiently from feeling things than they do when they think or meditate. It is very seldom that you will work with an athlete that can turn visual images into action.

Therefore, the touch "hands-on" technique is one of the best teaching methods a coach can use to enhance the learning process. During the "hands-on" learning sessions, the player must see the skill demonstrated properly, then he must feel his body perform it correctly by you touching and guiding his movements. You are aiding the player by enhancing his body awareness process to feel right. Repetitiously, as he continues to feel how to move correctly, he will successfully duplicate that remembered feeling alone in competition. This is the NEUROMUSCULAR MEMORY process.

"Hands-on" is the arrival destination. INFORM, INSTRUCT, and INSPIRE are the vehicles moving you down the road. Once you have arrived and identified what you need to give the player to enhance his potential, HANDS-ON must be the technique used by you to accelerate the learning process.

EXAMPLE

Player A has an IQ of 150 and can tell you all about good pitching mechanics, but he has trouble standing on the mound. Player B is from the ghetto and sometimes he doesn't even know that he is moving correctly. But, Player B moves efficiently because his body enables him to do it. Player B is FEELING and DOING SMART rather than thinking smart.

PERFORMANCE ANALYSIS

Coach, as you inform, instruct, and inspire, you must analyze your players' talents. Determine their strengths and weaknesses. How?...

If there is an important difference in what the young player is negatively doing and what is required of him to do, then as his coach, you have to synthesize all the previous information we have provided you and INFORM, INSTRUCT, and INSPIRE. Direct the three "I's" towards changing the player so he can maximize his potential resulting in better performances. If an important difference does not exist, then you have to reinforce and support continuously what is positively taking place.

Again, as a coach you have to continuously assess which form of action is appropriate. Am I going to INFORM, INSTRUCT or INSPIRE to change performance, or am I going to reinforce and support the player's current performance. Many times just leaving the situation alone is fine. Don't over-coach.

EXAMPLE

Coach A's team played poorly in three straight games. He hypothesized that his players played poorly because they were not motivated. Coach A then decided to conduct a performance analysis on his team. He watched several practices from the grandstand while the assistant coaches conducted the daily practices. First, after he had evaluated himself and his assistants, then his team, the composite analysis revealed that there was a real difference between the players' ACTUAL and DESIRED performance. Specifically, the analysis showed that the team knew how to execute, but they were not performing up to expectation. Coach A concluded that instruction was not what his team needed. His team needed inspiration.

Therefore, when you conduct a player performance analysis, you must determine why the players are failing. Locate the problem and address your coaching efforts towards finding a specific solution. If the players are performing up to expectation, then reinforce.

REINFORCEMENT

Coach, you should understand that when you instruct, you do not always have to try and "reinvent the wheel." But sometimes you do have to grease it a bit---INFORM, INSTRUCT, and INSPIRE. Remember, not all teaching and coaching has to be with brand new information---there can be REINFORCEMENT.

There are two kinds of reinforcement: positive and negative. Positive reinforcement produces desired behaviors. Negative reinforcement retards the learning process and produces ill feelings of self-esteem and/or disrespect toward the coach.

YOUR RIGHTEOUS CHARACTER ROLE MODEL IS THE BEST POSITIVE REINFORCEMENT ENHANCER YOU CARRY WITH YOU.

Before the season, make out a behavioral list. List all the behaviors that you want to instill within your players. Refer to it weekly. When any player behaves properly, reinforce this acceptable behavior. Also have a skill check list. When a player performs a skill correctly, reinforce this positive behavior, especially if he is trying his best and is showing steady improvement. **ALWAYS REWARD EFFORT!**

OBSTACLES

As you plan for practices and games, you must identify the obstacles and roadblocks that stand in your way. Ask, why haven't you been able to reach a particular objective or goal, why aren't the players performing to their potentials, and what possibly is getting in the way as you try to implement your working plan. Again, remember, PROBLEM IDENTIFICATION IS HALF THE SOLUTION.

Ask, what are the solutions for each of these obstacles. What needs to be done? You just can't show up and coach. As you search for the solutions, keep in mind that your young players are kids, not adults. They cannot act or perform like adults. The better you become at informing, instructing and inspiring, solutions will appear and obstacles will be defeated.

WINDOW OF OPPORTUNITY

Coach, your job now is to synthesize all the information presented and determine your DIRECTION. In summary, you have created objectives and goals, and analyzed your daily, weekly and seasonal tasks based on your players' performances and needs while gathering good information from this text. You have created your own *Coaching Manual For Success*.

You are now ready to apply your information and work with your team. You are ready to coach. As you begin the coaching process, again, you must MATCH-UP your knowledge with your positive behavioral character to achieve four important goals:

1. To enhance player behavioral capabilities and performances.
2. To create a synergy of team play.
3. To create an injury-free environment.
4. To create a fun and learning baseball environment.

This matching-up process is the key to successful coaching.

You must understand that this "marriage" of KNOWLEDGE with POSITIVE BEHAVIOR is a continuous journey in your coaching life. You should never lose the desire to improve. You must constantly search for new research-proven information as you continuously fine tune your "role model" behavior.

This journey is a never ending self-improvement and growth process. As you become more successful and experienced, this matching-up process will become meaningful and clearly defined. You will come to fully understand that the matching-up process is none other than a "window of opportunity."

As you travel down this journey, gaining knowledge, wisdom and experience, new opportunity windows will open for you. These windows come in many sizes or shapes, such as:

- Working with different age groups.
- Working with all-star caliber players.
- Recognition---rewarded for your success, by being asked to give clinics, or asked to give individualized instruction.

OVER-COACHING

Coach, be aware that at one time or another you may over-coach. Instruction, learning, and change are unjustified and often unnecessary when things are going right. If the pieces are fitting together, instruction, learning or change may or may not be needed.

"If it isn't broken, don't fix it." During the game, you must let the players play. Let them succeed or fail on their own. Naturally, you will coach during the game. But always remember, experience is a great teacher---SOMETIMES IT IS BETTER TO SIT AND WATCH!

PLANNING YOUR WORK
AND
WORKING YOUR PLAN

House's Six Steps for Daily Planning

- Step one is a two-parter. Part A is to determine the area(s) in which your young players' need improvement. In planning for today's practice, analyze last night's game performance or yesterday's practice performance and determine player weaknesses and improvement areas. You will have assessed each player's present status and his potential. Now, you have an evaluative basis to plan specific practice drills and techniques to prepare your team for competition.

Once you have constructed your daily plan, then you must determine how to implement this plan. The implementation proceedings are Part B. You should have a list of possible methods you could use when teaching your young players. Every home has several entrances into the living room . . . **Not every player receives INFORMATION, INSTRUCTION and INSPIRATION in the same manner. Determine the best methods of instruction for each individual player.**

You will recognize when you begin to individualize instruction to the specific needs of each player, you will not be treating everyone the same. What works for one player might not work for another. Your players come to you with individual differences and needs. Your job is to give them specific guidance to improve their performances as you help them reach their genetic potential. No way can you treat all your players the same way---as the old adage would like us to believe or do.

⑪ *COACHING TIP*

Remember, baseball is a team game made up of individuals. The individual is more important than the whole (team).

- Quick and clean workouts. The old wear and tear theory is outdated. Skill development is accelerated by lot of repetitions in short workouts. Each workout must have a focus, a lot of action, and tangible and obtainable objectives.

- Daily workouts must be conducted in a positive atmosphere. This positive atmosphere begins with your role model image. Besides your positive behavior, establish a positive communication exchange with each player. Use your "bag" of affirmations. Again, AFFIRMATIONS are positive statements---coach to athlete, athlete to coach, coach to self, and athlete to self.

- As you are constructing your daily practice, plan for possible obstacles and roadblocks. Be prepared to adjust. Always have additional equipment available and a list of sport-specific drills ready to use to meet the unforeseeable problem.

⚾ *COACHING TIP*

HAVING LOST SIGHT OF OUR OBJECTIVE, WE'VE DOUBLED OUR EFFORT TO GET THERE! Seventy percent of coaching time and effort is spent evaluating athletic performances---identifying the primary problem and/or obstacle and arriving at it's correct solution. Determine specifically, what needs to be done to solve the problem! TREAT THE ILLNESS, NOT THE SYMPTOM.

- It's not how hard a team or coach works, it's how smart they work.

- Restate solutions as positive present tense supportive affirmations. Supportive affirmations are so necessary for a young athlete's self-confidence, self-esteem, and self-worth.

⚾ *COACHING TIP*

Devise a seasonal calendar. All practices and games with their corresponding goals and objectives are listed on the calendar. From the calendar, you will create your daily practices and game plans.

Application: Planning Practices

Every practice should have a statement of mission or purpose. This statement will reflect the coach's philosophy and ethics as to the way he approaches his coaching plan.

Every practice should have objectives that follow the statement of purpose. These are daily and weekly obtainable statements, or mini-goals that help you reach the overall goals.

Every practice should contain strategies and tactics. Ethics is the day-to-day operation of setting up fundamental skill stations and specific-skill drills as you plan your work and work your plan for workouts and game preparations.

⚾ COACHING TIP

The key to successful planning is to keep in mind while you are developing your plan of action, you want to work with the strengths that you have. Put kids where they can succeed. Determine an area that has a high degree of success potential for each player. Then, put him into that spot so he can improve and work on that potential. Never ask a player to perform something in a game that he has not prepared for or is incapable of executing.

Every practice should begin with the following SEQUENTIAL WARM-UP:

General Warm-up

- Jog for 5 minutes.
- Stretch head-to-foot for 10 minutes.

Specific Warm-up

- Football throw (pee pee ball) for 5 minutes.
- Short-long toss with baseball for 5 minutes, all throws are on a line (one-hop long toss), no lobbing or lofting of the baseball. Now that the arm is warm, you must continue with throwing drills: infield-outfield, and/or bullpen work. After you have done all the needed throwing for the day, then you can have hitting drills and/or baserunning drills.

⚾ *COACHING TIP*

- *Never warm-up the arm and then immediately go into hitting or baserunning and then come back to throwing drills. This poor planning could cause a possible arm injury after the arm has cooled down.*

- *Baseball is a ballistic or anaerobic sport. Every play takes less than 15 seconds. Therefore, run-sprint your players. Interval sprints of 30 to 60 yards will produce anaerobic training effects.*

During practice rotate players by groups. Move your players from one drill station to another. Also, during practice rotate your coaches into stations. Organize your daily plan so that you utilize the strengths of your assistant coaches. Position yourself and your coaches at various drill stations for thorough instruction and organizational purposes.

EXAMPLE

Hitting is the most difficult skill to teach and execute. You should have the following hitting stations:

- Tee.
- Soft/hard toss.
- TWO batting practice areas---behind home plate and behind 3rd base (construct semi-portable netted batting cage) or indoor batting cage.

At each hitting station, there is a coach who has been taught to teach that skill in harmony within the overall hitting-coaching philosophy.

Every practice should have the following defensive stations:

- Football-throwing mechanics.
- Infielders-ground balls.
- Outfielders-fly balls and ground balls.
- Infield-outfield combination---simulate game defensive plays.

Every practice should have baserunning stations.

Young players must learn how to run properly. Examples of possible baserunning stations are as follows:

- Running technique stations---run through first base.
- Run the bases.
- Base stealing---stealing 2nd base, 3rd base, and home.

Every practice should have the following hitting stations:

- Bunting-sacrifice and drag bunts.
- Tee and/or soft-hard toss.
- Visual tracking station---learn how to track a pitch and take a pitch while learning the strike zone.
- Again, batting practice from two locations---behind the plate and behind 3rd base.

Suggestions for working your pitchers:

- Warm-up the pitcher as previously suggested. A pitcher should throw his bullpen immediately after he warms up. The bullpen should last no longer than 10 minutes. If he throws once a week, one bullpen between starts is enough.

- **If your pitcher plays another position, then have him throw the bullpen AFTER infield-outfield practice.** This will put less strain on the arm than if he throws the bullpen first then goes into infield/outfield practice.

- **After throwing the bullpen, shut him down.** No more throwing for the day. We favor icing the arm for a MAXIMUM of 20 minutes after he throws a bullpen or in a game. Research suggests that there are advantages of icing the arm.

- The worst position-pitcher combination is the catcher-pitcher. Remember, the catcher throws more than any other player. If it is at all possible, NEVER pitch your catcher. If you are going to use the catcher as your stopper (reliever) warm him up before he takes his beginning inning mandatory 5-7 warm-up pitches. Ice his arm after every bullpen and after a pitched game.

During your weekly practice, you should have a game simulation practice. Play a modified game.

Vary your practices. Have player input. And make your practices FUN!

> **PERFECT PRACTICES MAKES PERMANENT!**

Application: Game Planning

Preparation for a game is totally different than for a practice. In practice, your preparation is for skill development and physical conditioning. **In a game, your planning is EXECUTION, NOT WINNING.**

BASEBALL IS A VISUAL SPORT. The pitcher throws to a stationary target and the hitter hits a moving target. Anything that you do to distract the players from these two main objectives will cause mental and physical problems.

When you are coaching from the coaching box, verbal encouragements or instructions are destructive. You have now placed the hitter or pitcher in the "physical-auditory channel" as he concentrates only on your instructions or reprimands, whichever the case may be. He is not centering visually on the ball or target. And above all other skills, the young pitcher and hitter must CENTER with every pitch.

Coach, if you give physical advice from the dugout as the hitter walks to the plate, again he will concentrate on your instructions, i.e. "keep your eye on the ball," "don't swing at the high pitch," "get extension," "keep your hands back," etc. Now at the plate, he will focus on his "physical channel" and not on his visual-tracking skills. Although you had good intentions, you now have harmfully distracted your hitter from visually concentrating while tracking the ball.

Visual research studies support the fact that if a player is concentrating on his body or his physical movement, it will hinder his visual-tracking system. ALL MOVEMENT BEGINS WITH THE VISUAL SYSTEM.

DeRenne's Laws of Competitive Performance

- **Never teach mechanics during a game.**
- **Put players in the visual system.**
- **Successful Performance = Confidence + Concentration + Relaxation.**
- **Confidence, concentration and relaxation are functions of PREPARATION.**

Practices are for skill development. Motor-Learning research reveals that it takes a good athlete between one to two weeks to correct a mechanical skill. How can you expect a young player to instantly improve his mechanical skills in an adrenalin situation under pressure? Therefore, in a game you and your assistant coaches should only give visual advice.

EXAMPLES

HITTERS

Did you see the ball as a beach ball, bigger and slower? Where was the pitch you swung at or hit? Are you centering on the ball as it comes out of the pitcher's hand, or staring out and looking at the whole pitcher?

PITCHERS

You should have your pitcher aim at a target with every warm-up throw. You should have your pitcher pick-up the target early before he strides forward to deliver the ball. During the conference out at the mound, do the following:

- Have your pitcher step off the mound, get his breath and clear his mind.
- After he knows what to do with the next pitch, he then steps back onto the mound and concentrates only on centering on the target.
- He must understand that his job is only to hit the target.
- In the wind-up or from the stretch, he should pick-up the target as early as possible. During the delivery, he should never take his eyes off the target.

During the game, the players on the bench should be quiet while concentrating on the game. From the bench, only words of encouragement toward teammates should be allowed by the coach. A bench coach should constantly be asking "game" and visual questions to the players. **You must keep the players "in" the game and help each player stay visual.**

Plan at least one inning in advance to warm-up your relief pitcher. If he is already in the game, don't assume he is warm. If he is going to hit in the half-inning before he pitches, find a way to warm him up. If he is an infielder or outfielder, instead of fielding throws before the inning, have a coach catch him at third base or along the side lines before the inning commences. Find a way to get him ready in case you have to use him in relief.

Offense

Offensively, every player must see how valuable he is in the offense. Remember, offensively the goal is to score runs. The hitter's objective is either to score a run himself, or to help produce a run. Teach players how to "manufacture" runs. Keep an offensive chart in the dugout to show the REAL value each player's time at bat was to the overall offense. The chart should include the following:

- Runs scored.
- RBI.
- Advanced baserunners.
- On base percentage.
- Hits.
- Scored runner.
- Clutch RBI (two out hit, RBI).
- Batting average.
- Clutch hitting chart (see next page).

> **IT IS THE QUALITY AT BAT THAT COUNTS, NOT THE BATTING AVERAGE.**

Defense

Each player must understand the importance of defense. Every player loves to hit more than anything else. You must stress the importance of "holding down the enemy." Young players have a difficult time adjusting to defense when they were unsuccessful at the plate. Here are some suggestions that will help your player make this difficult transition:

- Keep a defensive chart in the dugout. Include:

  - Number of good throws, pickups, catches, etc.
  - 2 out defensive play with runners on.
  - Thrown out runners.
  - Award the defensive game breaker play of the game.
  - Remember, get into the practice of always commending every player for their defensive effort and successful plays.

- In practices, always stress hustle and defense. Reward the hustler and defensive practice player of the week.

- During the awards banquet, you should have offensive, defensive, improvement, sportsmanship and academic awards.

When making out your lineup, put the players in the order that they will most likely succeed.

During the game, NEVER ask a player to execute a difficult task if he has not practiced that skill or if, in fact, he is not skilled enough to execute the task. Give your players every chance to succeed. DON'T ASK OR EXPECT MORE FROM THEM THAN WHAT THEY ARE CAPABLE OF GIVING.

EXAMPLE

You put the squeeze bunt on with your eighth or ninth batter to win the game. But, during the week you have not had any bunting practice. If this particular young player is not a very good bunter, then the odds of success are not in his favor. If he fails, it is not his fault.

⚾ *COACHING TIP*

Never relate poor game performance to preceding poor practices. If there were poor practices before a game, then it was a coaching fault, not the players' fault. The coaches are in control---blame yourselves.

Box Score

Baseball is a team sport made-up of individuals. In your youth program the individual players are KIDS. Each young player has his own individual character and performance level. He is not an adult. Do not expect him to act mature and play as an adult.

Your job is to improve the character and skill level of every player you coach. Accept him as he is. Take him from where he is to a higher level of performance.

In order to raise every player's level and build his character, you must plan for every player to have some degree of success during practices and in games. Specifically, you must assess the needs of every player and create short-term and long-term objectives to meet those player needs.

Coaching is a journey. The player's journey with you must be positive and rewarding. During this journey, you must provide the players with an enjoyable and learning atmosphere, or you will hinder the growth of your team. A positive and rewarding journey begins, continues and ends with good INFORMATION, INSTRUCTION and INSPIRATION.

CLUTCH BATTING CHART

Player	H & R	K	SB	Sacrifice Bunt	Sacrifice Fly	Adv. Run.	Scoring R. 2/3B < 2 Out	On Base	RBI	Runs Scored	Batting Avg.

III
Mom and the
Single Parent

"A Mother is she, who can take the place of all others, but whose place no one else can take."

Mom, this chapter is for you. You are a very important person in the baseball development of your son. We feel you can help your son with his athletic development more than you realize. For this reason, we have dedicated this chapter to our moms and to single parents.

We will provide you with general and sometimes specific suggestions or ideas. Mom, you are special. Get involved with your son's athletic development and you will enjoy your special relationship with him even more.

NUTRITION

Eat to Compete

During our years as players, we were always told to run a lot. This was to have strong legs and to keep in shape through the long season. Nothing, however, was ever mentioned about what type of fuel we should put into our bodies to complement the running.

Today, we know that running is important for its cardiovascular-respiratory affect, i.e. to increase stamina by increasing blood flow and oxygen to the muscles. We have also learned through research that, in effect, "you are what you eat." A person cannot think well or work well if he has not eaten well.

A good analogy compares your body to an automobile. To make it run efficiently, it must be fueled with the best possible gas and oil. Likewise, your body must have the purest blood circulating to its moveable parts. The composition of the blood depends on the food we eat. If you eat properly, normal blood is generated and the heart, liver, other organs, and muscles function as they should. Under these conditions, inefficiency is practically impossible.

If you take two pitchers of equal ability with the same workout program, the one most conscientious about his diet will have more energy to sustain peak performance levels. Why? A skilled athlete must have good timing, accuracy of movement, and the proper degree of muscular contraction during competition. For a muscle to contract, it must have an energy source called ATP. In the presence of oxygen, the muscle gets all the ATP it needs. The supply of oxygen in a muscle is solely a function of blood flow through the tissue. Therefore, if the blood flow is restricted for any reason, muscle fatigue results.

Nutrients

Strength, power and endurance come only through physical training. A proper diet provides the necessary raw materials that allow the training to build and run the human machine. There are six classes of nutrients:

- Carbohydrates.
- Proteins.
- Fats.
- Vitamins.
- Minerals.
- Water.

Carbohydrates

- Carbohydrates should be 60-70% of the calorie intake.
- A high-carbohydrate diet is especially important to the athlete in training who works out 3-6 hours a day.
- At least 60% of calorie intake should be from **complex carbohydrates** (starches and fibers) in order to keep the glycogen stores filled.
- The body converts complex carbohydrates to glucose for energy or to glycogen for energy storage in the liver and muscle tissues. These glycogen stores can be increased in specific muscle tissue. This is called "carbo-loading."
- If you are eating a high-carbohydrate diet, even muscles severely emptied of glycogen due to training can be adequately refilled within 24 hours.
- Fiber is not absorbed but is essential for gastrointestinal functioning. Low-fiber diets have been associated with many diseases including diverticulosis, constipation, heart disease, cancer of the colon and diabetes.

Sources of Complex Carbohydrates

Whole Grains

Cereals and breads, oatmeal, cold cereals (low in sugar, i.e. oats, shredded wheat), wheat germ, plain granola, buckwheat, rye, corn breads, bran muffins, crackers, pancakes, etc.

Pastas

Especially made with whole wheat, soy, or semolina flours, spaghetti, macaroni, noodles, pasta salad, etc.

Other Starches

Potatoes (preferably baked), brown rice, poi, breadfruit, tapioca, beans.

Vegetables

Peas, lentils, green beans, asparagus, broccoli, brussel sprouts, cabbage, carrots, celery, corn, garlic, all leafy greens (lettuce, etc.), mushrooms, onions, peas, peppers, spinach, squash, sweet potatoes, tomatoes, taro.

Fruits (High in Simple Sugars)

Apples, oranges, bananas, papaya, mangoes, pineapple, grapefruit, peaches, nectarines, avocadoes, coconuts, cherries, figs, kiwi, raisins, watermelon, and all natural fruit juices.

⊕ *COACHING TIP*

Simple sugar carbohydrates such as cookies, cakes, sodas, candy, etc., negatively affect performance. Ingestion of concentrated sugars ("sugar rush") up to 45 minutes before competition or training results in decreased performance because of a tendency of the pancreas to secrete insulin. This higher insulin level prevents the body from using fat and, therefore, glycogen must be used exclusively. Fructose (sugars in fruits) produces a lower insulin response than does sucrose (white sugar) for most individuals. Sugars are also low or deficient in protein, vitamins, minerals and dietary fiber. Simple sugars may cause cramps, nausea, gas and bloating.

Protein

- Protein should be 15-20% of your calorie intake. Even during intense training and build-up, protein intake above these levels are unnecessary and converted into fat!
- Protein in the diet furnishes material for new growth, to maintain and repair tissue and to build body proteins.
- Protein is needed for formation of materials that transport fat.
- Protein helps maintain the proper amount of fluid in the blood and tissues.
- Protein also provides energy if there is a shortage of the other energy nutrients.

Sources of Protein

Meats

Fish, shrimp, clams, sardines, tuna, salmon, chicken, turkey (nutritious), red meats, (high in fat)---beef, veal, lamb, pork (ham), bacon.

Dairy Products

Milk, eggs, cheese, yogurt, mayonnaise, custards, cottage cheese.

Other Proteins

Nuts, beans, (refried, baked, Portuguese bean soup).

Plant Protein

Soybeans, peas, beans, nuts.

⚾ COACHING TIP

Because animal protein takes a long time to digest, it should be avoided the night before and the day of competition. Eat protein AFTER the performance to help muscles build and repair themselves.

Fats

- Fats are found in meats (animal sources), eggs, milk, cheese, fried foods, butter, margarine, avocados, coconuts, salad dressings, oils, mayonnaise, and nuts.
- A certain amount of fat is essential in the diet.
- A high-fat diet is associated with many diseases.

Vitamins and Minerals

- Today's athlete should begin to realize that correct selection of food can more directly affect performance than taking vitamin and mineral supplements.
- It is believed that taking a supplement increases performance only because the athlete has increased mental confidence.
- There is also a question as to how much the body readily absorbs and uses these supplements.

Water

- Drink 8-10 cups a day (about 2 liters).
- Add orange, lemon (or other citrus fruits) to the glass of water for a nutritious fruit drink.
- Weigh yourself before and after exercise then replace your water loss. Drink two cups per pound of body weight loss.

Five Factors that Contribute to Muscle Fatigue

- Food allergies.
- Enzyme deficiency.
- Refined carbohydrate, protein, and fat ingestions before competition.
- Anaerobic exercise to excess; i.e. calisthenics, sprinting, weight training.
- A training schedule that is too vigorous and does not allow for muscle recovery.

Four Factors that Contribute to Muscle Contraction

- Compatible foods.
- Adequate enzyme intake.
- Complex carbohydrates.
- Aerobic exercise; i.e. jogging, swimming, bicycling, jumping rope, aerobic dancing, etc.

During the last decade, doctors discovered that food allergies can cause symptoms in many parts of the body. They have also found that these symptoms can be dramatically relieved when one or more allergy producing foods are eliminated from the diet. Another interesting phenomenon is that the foods that cause a child's symptoms are often his favorites---he may crave them and eat them several times a day!

St. Louis allergist, Dr. William Bryan, developed a test for food allergies that studies the impact of the allergy-causing substance on the white blood cells, our body's defense system against disease. He found that the food reaction seen in the white blood cells aggravates most illnesses. Those foods that destroy an athlete's white blood cells should be eliminated from his diet.

The Two Types of Food Allergies

- A fixed or permanent allergy is usually caused by uncommon foods like strawberries, lobster, or shrimp. Skin rashes, hives, or other violent skin eruptions are typical of this type of allergic reaction. Common foods like chocolate, eggs, or peanuts can sometimes cause the same problems.
- A hidden or variable allergy, while more common, is harder to recognize and is often overlooked. Characteristic symptoms of such allergies include fatigue, irritability, pale color, dark circles under the eyes, stuffy nose, stomachache, headache, leg ache, and mouth breathing. Foods commonly involved with such reactions include milk, corn, chocolate, wheat, egg, cane sugar, citrus fruits, beans, beef, and pork. Remember, when the diet is deficient, allergies and illnesses are apt to occur.

Enzymes

When food is cooked above 118 degrees Fahrenheit, the enzymes are destroyed. This means that the pancreas, salivary glands, stomach, and intestines must come to the rescue and furnish digestive enzymes to break down protein, carbohydrates, and fats in cooked foods. Eventually, there will be a deficiency of enzymes because the body must rob enzymes from glands, muscles, nerves, and blood to help in the chemical breakdown of food. Many researchers feel that this enzyme deficiency is the real cause of allergies and disease.

Cooked food passes more slowly through the digestive tract than raw food, and as a result, can set up allergic reactions including gas, heartburn, headaches, stuffy nose, and eye problems. The best natural source of digestive enzymes should come from eating raw vegetables with cooked foods. Pineapple and papaya are excellent sources of enzymes that work on proteins. Aspergillus plants have the enzymes to help digest proteins, fats, and carbohydrates.

Foods to Avoid

- Refined carbohydrates (simple sugars) should be avoided or at least limited at mealtime, including sugar in the sugar bowl, candy, soft drinks, cookies, doughnuts, canned juices, chocolate, maple syrup, ice cream, and most junk foods. Some of the foods mom thought were good for you, such as peanut butter, ketchup, breakfast cereals, and many canned fruits and vegetables also have hidden sugar. As mentioned earlier, this sugar gets into the bloodstream, rapidly giving the body a quick burst of energy, but one that doesn't last long. After a short time, the body becomes jittery and suffers a letdown of muscle fatigue---actually to a point lower than before the food was eaten. This becomes a problem for the person who eats a second round of refined carbohydrates for another quick pickup, as the cycle repeats itself.
- Fried foods: french fries, hamburgers, fried chicken, potato chips, etc.
- Alcohol.
- Mayonnaise salads (macaroni, potato).
- White rice, it is usually stripped of most of it's fiber and nutrients.
- Red meats: beef, port, spam, etc.

Energy Foods

Complex carbohydrates, on the other hand, contain time-released sugar. Because this sugar comes into the bloodstream gradually, the body's muscles work better because energy is sustained over a longer period of time. This gives the player the fuel to perform for a full game.

Remember that the body burns carbohydrates first, then proteins or amino acids. The best sources of animal protein include meat, fish, poultry, eggs, milk, and milk products. Good sources of plant protein include soybeans, peas, beans, and nuts. Because animal protein takes a long time to digest, it should be avoided on the day of competition. Eat protein after the game to help muscles build and repair themselves.

Good Snacks

- Carrot sticks, apples, bananas, whole wheat crackers with cheese, popcorn (low salt, no butter), bran muffins, celery, raisins.
- Try to limit your snacks to foods high in complex carbohydrates to ensure a high carbohydrate diet.

Fat

Fat is burned by the body and is the major cause of oxygen debt. To burn fat effectively, an athlete must exercise aerobically (steady and non-stop 25 minute exercise for three alternate days).

If a player is not exercising properly, the oxygen supply to his muscles is inadequate, and his body performs sluggishly. The portion of the fuel that is not burned completely is called lactic acid and it impedes muscle contraction, increases fatigue, and eventually causes cramping. Fat can have four times as many blood vessels as an equivalent amount of muscle tissue, so excess fat really puts a strain on the heart. Fat intake comes from meat, dairy products, oils, nut butters, avocados, and olives. Eating too much fat can cause obesity, skin problems, hypoglycemia, diabetes, and many other disease symptoms.

What Foods Should or
Should Not Be Eaten During Training?

- Do not eat sugar substitutes, refined carbohydrates, canned foods, fried foods, alcoholic beverages, coffee, or tea.
- Do eat from the four basic food groups, including meat, eggs, fruit, vegetables, nuts, and whole grain breads and cereals.
- Eat a good, high-protein breakfast to stabilize the blood sugar level and a moderate, low-fat lunch of complex carbohydrates and some protein. The evening meal should be the lightest, consisting mainly of complex carbohydrates and protein.
- Take a good multivitamin/mineral supplement to balance nutritional loss from poor soil, transportation, storage, processing and preparation.

What Should a Player Eat on Game Days?

- Eat three hours before the game if possible. The meal should be high in complex carbohydrates, i.e. brown rice, potatoes, pasta, or cooked cereals---and low in protein because proteins are not easily burned. Stay away from fats, oils, or refined carbohydrates, i.e. no butter, whole milk, cheese, salad oil, avocados, cakes, candies, sodas, or ice cream.
- Drink plenty of water between meals to prevent dehydration. Try to limit fluid intake at mealtime to eight ounces to prevent dilution of enzymes that allow for proper digestion and absorption of the meal. Drink water in moderation throughout the game to help prevent dehydration and muscle fatigue.

What's a Good Snack
for Between Games in a Doubleheader?

Foods

Fresh fruit (eat anytime during the day), fresh vegetables, water or juice-packed fruit, whole rye crackers, rice cakes, whole wheat pita bread, water-packed tuna, and hot cereal.

Liquids

Water, fruit juices without added sugar, and vegetable juices.

Other

Bee pollen mixed in a glass of fruit juice. Pollen is one of nature's richest foods, overflowing with natural vitamins, minerals, and proteins in the proportional amounts that are so necessary to digestion and assimilation. Local bee pollen is the best---it has long been recommended by doctors as a nutritional supplement for respiratory allergies.

The tough daily schedules of athletes, coaches, and parents make rigid adherence to good nutritional habits difficult. High cost and inconvenience and fast food outlets don't help. Be flexible, but be smart-- considering everything, investing in your body makes good sense, especially when you realize it's the only body you have!

SKILL DEVELOPMENT

Every day that you can play and work with your son is another day that he's closer to reaching his athletic potential. You have no way of knowing what his potential is. If you make a commitment to him and yourself that you will help his development then at least you can look at yourself in the mirror the day he leaves home and say, "I really tried, I gave my all."

At Home

Mom, here are some helpful suggestions you can personally do to help your son develop his baseball skills:

Playing Catch

- Learn how to play catch from your coach.
- Use soft imitation baseballs or tennis balls.
- Make sure you and your son have the right size gloves. You want to develop your son's hands, not have the glove doing all the work (small gloves are best).
- Emphasize catching the ball with two hands.

Fielding

- Find out from your coach fielding progression drills you can do at home.
- Begin by rolling the balls to your sons as they catch bare handed (wear batting gloves). This will develop their soft hands.
- Throw a variety of fly balls to your sons. Make them learn to go back on a fly ball correctly.
- In your driveway or backyard, hit ground balls. Use rubber or soft baseballs.

GLOVE SIZE

A young player's glove must be as small as possible, not adult size. A small glove allows the player to develop soft hands and improve his catching mechanics. The glove on the left is an adult size---too big!

Fielding

Initially, a young player should learn to field ground balls with bare hands, or batting gloves. Use different size balls and softer balls when using this drill.

Hitting

- Use a traffic cone for a batting tee. Use soft imitation baseballs and hit against a fence. Put an old rug, etc., on the fence so as not to ruin the fence.
- Learn to toss soft baseballs as he hits against a fence. Ask your coach for instructions.
- Buy the commercial Swing N' Hit baseball hitting device. This is a rubber baseball attached to a cord that you can swing in a circle in the air as your son stands away from you and hits the moving baseball. Use this in your backyard or on your driveway. This is a great hitting device to teach your son how to track (follow) the ball. Plus, you do not have to pitch to him or chase after the baseballs.
- If you have space and money, put up a netted batting cage in your backyard.
- Buy a ping pong table. This sport teaches eye-hand coordination.
- Play Whiffle ball with your son.
- Play racquetball, tennis and badminton with your son. Again, these sports will develop eye-hand coordination and help develop his lateral quickness for defense.

- Pitch baseballs, soft baseballs and bean bags against a fence while your son tracks these moving objects as he learns how to take a pitch.
- For all hitting drills, place your son into the stride box.

Traffic Cone Tee

Swing n' Hit

The Stride Box

The stride box controls the length and direction of the hitter's stride.

Hitting/Pitching Net

In Hawaii, most youth teams have a multi-purpose hitting/pitching net. It is used in practices and before games.

Pitching

- Buy a portable baseball plate and catch your son.
- Hang a tire from a tree as a target for your son. He should try and throw footballs through the tire.
- Have someone construct a rectangle wooden strike zone with cut out circle targets. Stand it against the rug covered chain link fence for control practice. Your son can pitch baseballs, soft baseballs, or even bean bags through the holes.

Strength and Speed Development

- Have your son do daily body resistance exercises: push-ups, dips, sit-ups, chin-ups, and pull-ups.
- Hang a chin-up bar inside the garage.
- Hang a boxing speed-bag inside the garage. This will help him develop eye-hand coordination and quick, strong hands.
- For speed, have your son run sprints. Run on flat ground and down slight inclines. Jump rope for quickness.
- In a backyard or community swimming pool, have him do kickboard and treading water exercises, and running in the pool for leg strength development.

Indoors

- Buy or rent instructional videos.
- Play darts, it develops the visual system.
- Practice hitting in the neighborhood gym.

At Night

- Go under the street lights so you can still play with your son after a full day's work.

At Your Condo

At your condo, you can do almost all of the above fundamental suggestions that someone else could do in a home.

- Use the driveways for playing catch, pitching and hitting drills. Select from the above list safe drills you can use for your particular living situation.

- DO NOT USE YOUR CONDO AS AN EXCUSE NOT TO PLAY OR WORK WITH YOUR SON OR DAUGHTER. GET CREATIVE!

- *Indoors*

    - Buy or rent instructional videotapes. You both can learn.
    - Put up a chin-up bar in his room.
    - Subscribe to baseball magazines.
    - Play darts, it develops the visual system.

- At night, play under the street lights.

- Go regularly to the recreational parks with all your homemade baseball equipment.

At the Park

Transport all your homemade equipment to the park in case the baseball fields are being used.

- Take your four-pole batting-pitching net for toss drills, soft toss drills, and bullpen work.
- Take rubber baseballs in case the ground is wet.
- If you want your son to pitch off the wet mound, construct a homemade pitching platform. It should consist of a plywood board covered with indoor-outdoor carpeting nailed to small wooden blocks. Lay the platform down the slope of the wet mound. He can throw on top of this pitching platform. If the plate area is wet, have another platform covering the catcher's area so you can still play catch with your son. He also can hit off this platform.
- Always have a variety of baseballs to use in all kinds of weather and for all kinds of facilities: regulation batting practice baseballs, old-tape baseballs, soft baseballs for indoors, and rubber baseballs. **NEVER THROW A BASEBALL AWAY, EVEN IF THE COVER HAS FALLEN OFF. TAPE IT WITH ATHLETIC TAPE AND USE IT FOR HITTING DRILLS.**

⚾ *COACHING TIP*

Mom, you may think these suggestions are a little extreme. Remember, if you are a typical mom on the go, the time you spend helping your son is very precious to the both of you. Therefore, never let the weather or crowded baseball areas prevent you from having fun with your son. PREPARE AND BE CREATIVE!

HOW MUCH DO YOU LOVE YOUR SON OR DAUGHTER? WE UNDERSTAND IT TAKES A SPECIAL MOM OR DAD TO IMPLEMENT THE ABOVE SUGGESTIONS. BUT IF YOU DO, YOUR SON OR DAUGHTER WILL REMEMBER YOUR EFFORTS FOR THE REST OF THEIR LIVES. THE SPIN-OFF AFFECT IS THAT THE TWO OF YOU WILL BE FRIENDS FOR A LIFETIME. LASTING IMPRESSIONS ARE FOREVER!

BEHAVIOR DEVELOPMENT

> **ALOHA MEANS GIVING WHILE NOT EXPECTING IN RETURN, AND WHEN RECEIVING, GIVE BACK!**

In Hawaii, there is a sense of family in the athletic communities, called Ohana. The team is a family. Not only do they play sports together, they participate in many other activities together.

Sometimes the coach becomes a "surrogate" family member. Moms, rely on the coach to help you with your son's behavioral development. The coach can provide your son with a father or authority figurehead. Many of our "local" coaches are actively involved in the overall home-baseball disciplining of their players. The players are given home and baseball responsibilities by the coach with approval from the Mom. Mom and coach should work together to help the player develop a good moral and stable character ("The Three R's").

```
CHARACTER   =    REAL, RESPONSIBILITY, RIGHT
              (Honesty)                 (vs. Wrong)
```

You must understand and accept that your coach may have a special influence over your son. Take advantage of this relationship. Seek as much help as possible. We all must do our part to keep our young players off the streets.

Research reveals that the number one deterrent against a young person turning toward a delinquent life is ATHLETICS. Sports and coaches HAVE SAVED more young people's lives from crime and social destruction than anything else in society.

We commend all youth coaches. You have an awesome responsibility and influence. Use this "power" constructively and help our Moms and single parents. They need you desperately!

NEVER USE CALISTHENICS AS A PUNISHMENT. You should help your son develop a positive attitude toward calisthenics and body resistance presses because he needs them for strength and flexibility development.

The coach can help you with your son's homework, home responsibilities, rules enforcement, family problems and discipline.

TEAM MOM

Every youth team must have a TEAM MOM. This special lady is the general of the team parents. She works closely with the coaching staff and alleviates organizational nuisances so the coaches can attend only to coaching.

Team Mom sets up the communication line with all parents on the team. This communication linkage consists of developing a telephone chain. She will recruit other moms, setting up a communication system to disseminate pertinent information.

Team Mom has many responsibility areas. These areas include: (1) medical, (2) liability, (3) disseminate information, and (4) planning social functions.

Medical

All players must have had a physical examination clearance to participate. The physical examination is required for participation and it must have been given within 6-months prior to the sport season. Team Mom keeps the records on file.

⓫ COACHING TIP

Coach, you should keep a small pocket medical notebook in your back pocket during practices and games. The contents must include:

1. Team Roster---home and business telephone numbers.
2. Specific medical problems certain players have---allergies, asthma, allergies to medications, prior serious injuries, etc.
3. Emergency telephone numbers.
4. Loose change for phone calls.

Team Mom organizes a water and ice schedule. At every practice and game there must be plenty of water for the team. A cooler of crushed ice in plastic bags must be present at every practice and game.

Team Mom takes care of the medical first aid kit. She checks the kit weekly to see if any medical supplies need replacing. Ask the local Red Cross or paramedics to help you stock the first aid kit. Carry loose change and the team telephone roster in the kit in case you need to make emergency phone calls.

You must have a team parent and/or coach trained in CPR and FIRST AID. This parent and/or coach must be present at all practices and games if possible. Note where all telephones are located at practices and games.

Minor treatments:
  R.I.C.E.---rest, ice, compression, and elevation.

LEGAL ASPECTS - CIVIL LITIGATION

Law

- The law deals with the fundamental principle of reasonable care.
- The younger the child, the higher your legal duty.
- Plaintiff's role: to acquire compensation and safer conditions.
- The league organization must carry liability insurance.

Instructions for Coaches

- Teach children at their competence level.
- Know growth characteristic (mental and physical) of children, therefore don't push child to point of injury.
- Always give safety instructions.
- Don't push children to jeopardize their future.
- Be conservative when there may be a question in your mind.

Supervision by Coaches

- When parents drop off their children, they are in your care. You must assume all responsibilities.
- Set procedures and consequences for pick-ups after practice.
- Do not designate anyone to supervise or take home a child after practice.

Facilities

- Inspect the playing area. Check for hazardous conditions.
- Notify, in writing, the official caretaker of any hazardous conditions.

Medical

- Require pre-participation medical exams before every sport.
- Parental approval and waiver forms are not legally binding.
- Know players' medical history. It is your responsibility to know medical problems.
- You should be certified in CPR and Standard First Aid by the American Red Cross.
- Have a First Aid kit ready.

⚾ *COACHING TIP*

Team Mom and the coaching staff should check all team equipment regularly. Before every practice and game, Team Mom, parents, and the coaching staff should walk around the field and check the field. They should pick up loose glass, sharp objects, cans, etc.

If the playing field is deemed dangerous---holes, fences need mending, etc., notify the caretaker in charge. If the city or county is responsible, notify their parks and recreation department supervisor in writing (sending letter certified is recommended) about the hazardous conditions. Document everything!

Again, you must have a parent or coach trained in CPR and Standard First Aid present at all practices and games. When an injury occurs during a practice or a game, this first aid parent is in charge until qualified medical personnel arrive on the scene.

BOX SCORE

No one is more important to the growth and development of children than mothers. "Feminism" is not an acceptable excuse to not play ball with your son or daughter. Get involved. He will remember your effort for a lifetime. With every catch and throw, you will be enhancing the family bonding process.

Section Two

FUNDAMENTALS

IV
Position Mechanics

"Baseball's fundamental movements are ballistic,
linear, rotational and lateral in nature.
Only the agile player survives."

--Dr. Coop DeRenne

We have decided to present to you the following old and new pertinent information concerning fundamentals. All the new information presented is based on research and proven intuitive experience, not opinion or tradition. Research "comes off the bench" to contribute new data concerning position biomechanics. Every position on the field has gone through some kind of mechanical change over the last ten years.

Before we discuss skill development, let's look at some principles of conditioning.

PHYSICAL CONDITIONING

Underlying Principle

Players must be fit to compete. During practices, provide your players with basic fitness exercises---warm-up, calisthenics, light jogging, and anaerobic sprints.

Principles of Conditioning

- Overload: How much stress is enough? When you increase distances, body resistances, intensity (rate of work), duration of work, and rest time must be increased.
- Intensity is more critical than duration.
- When teaching a new skill or correcting a mechanical flaw, regression precedes improvement.
- Fatigue impairs learning.
- Fitness: easier to maintain than attain.
- Individual Difference: Treat all players differently. Children are born different, and experience different rates of growth, etc.
- Motivation: Children need to be motivated to learn.
- More endurance work early in the year, more high intensity work as season approaches.

THROWING MECHANICS

Throwing is the number one abusive skill in baseball. The majority of young players do not know how to throw. All around the country this is a truism. Youngsters can't throw because: (1) poor information, (2) neglect on the parents and coaches part to teach them proper throwing mechanics, and (3) the regulation baseball is too heavy and big for most children's throwing hands.

Throwing is a combination of BALANCE, DIRECTION, and WEIGHT TRANSFER. Master the throwing motion through repetition and reinforcement so that neuromuscular memory replaces conscious mental effort.

Throwing mechanics are the same for all positions. Whether you are an infielder, outfielder, catcher, or pitcher, the physical act of throwing is the same for all players. First, coaches, think of the body as being divided exactly in half with the throwing side identified as the "strong" or back side and the glove side as the "directional" or front side. Second, there are five basic rules of mechanics to follow when throwing a baseball. They are as follows:

- Glove side is your directional side. Wherever you are on a baseball field, you follow your glove side when you throw a baseball.
- As you receive the ball, bury ("ride") the ball into your chest area. As you begin to throw, close off your body so you are facing your target sideways by stepping or pivoting on your back side foot (right foot if you are right-handed). Therefore, the front side foot, knee, hip, shoulder, and glove are pointing toward the target with the ball drawn into the chest area. All position players must do this as they throw the baseball.
- After you receive any baseball---playing catch, a fly ball, or ground ball---and pulled your hands to your chest area, your hands must break apart to throw the baseball by turning your thumbs underneath. This forces you to get your elbows up on every throw. As you break thumbs underneath (fingers on top of the ball), drop the hand down toward the ground so the arm is fully extended. Then the arm will automatically continue in a long figure eight route with a shoulder high throwing elbow.
- As you turn your thumbs underneath, you want the elbows to get shoulder height during the throwing arc as the arm accelerates forward. You want both elbows even with the shoulders. Think of a wheel with your head as the hub and your elbow-arms are the spokes of the wheel. You will throw around this wheel, whirling and rotating the body as you accelerate the ball forward with shoulder height elbows.

- Weight Transfer: Coach, the head determines if we have a good weight transfer. As you accelerate the arm forward, take your head out and over your landing leg foot. Think about burying your nose into the catcher's glove as you step toward the target while releasing the baseball. This will automatically free the body to have a proper weight transfer. You are transferring your center of gravity from the backside to the front side by using your head to lead the weight transfer. The key to positive reinforcement will be as you finish releasing the ball, look down and see if your head is directionally pointing at the target and that it is out and over the landing leg.

⚾ *COACHING TIP*

At the very beginning of the season after you have filled your roster, bring all the dads and moms out to the first week of practice. During this first week of practice, teach the parents how to throw. Dads play more catch with their sons than anyone else. If they throw improperly, then the young player will mimic dad's poor mechanics.

CATCHING & THROWING SEQUENCE

A. PREPARATION
(1) square stance; (2) center on target;
(3) prepare glove; (4) use two hands.

B. *THE CATCH*
(1) body behind the ball
(2) use two hands
(3) "ride" the ball into chest

C. *BEGIN TO THROW*
(1) balanced stance
(2) eyes on target
(3) hands together

D. *PIVOT & LINE UP*
(1) back leg pivots so body
    lines up to target
(2) front foot, knee, shoulder
    and glove line up to target

E. *SEPARATION*
(1) break hands with thumbs
    underneath
(2) follow glove, take front
    side to target
(3) wrist on top of ball
(4) drop down and swing up

F. GOAL POST POSITION

(1) *high elbow (shoulder height)*
(2) *baseball facing opposite direction before accelerating forward*
(3) *glove leads throw*
(4) *figure "8" arm route*
(5) *linear step to target*

G. SIDE VIEW: GOAL POST

H. ACCELERATION

(1) *arm follows glove, "take & replace," (glove, then ball)*
(2) *rotation begins at the hips, then trunk, last shoulders*
(3) *eyes on target*
(4) *fingers on top of ball*

I. BALL RELEASE

(1) *high elbow, firm wrist behind the ball: 12-6 o'clock rotation*
(2) *complete rotation*
(3) *nose (weight shift at target)*
(4) *snap fingers and wrist straight down*
(5) *head over front knee*

Playing Catch

Coaches and parents, again, make sure you buy your son the right size glove for his position. Most young players use a glove that is way too big for them. If your son is an infielder, make sure he uses a very small glove, one that is a little larger than his hand. Do not buy the young outfielder or pitcher an adult size glove. An oversized glove reinforces poor catching mechanics. **IF THE GLOVE IS TOO BIG, THEN THE GLOVE WILL ACTUALLY BE DOING THE CATCHING AND NOT THE PLAYER.** The young player will never develop good catching mechanics and "soft" hands, if the glove is too big for him---**IF THE TOOL IS NOT RIGHT, THE PLAYER IS NOT BRIGHT!** Always play catch with two hands.

As the two players play catch, you must make sure they follow proper throwing mechanics. The football is the best throwing-reinforcing device there is. YOU CAN NOT MAKE A FOOTBALL SPIRAL AND THROW IT INCORRECTLY. If the player spirals a football then his throwing mechanics are correct.

When the advanced players are playing catch, they should "crow-hop" while they receive and throw the ball. This drill will reinforce quick feet and hands. YOU DON'T THROW WITH YOUR HANDS, YOU THROW WITH YOUR FEET. Your feet always lead your glove and body toward the target. Therefore, since baseball is a ballistic game, learn to throw correctly, accurately, and quickly.

🌑 *COACHING TIP*

> *Many young infielders have small hands. Even though you find a small infielder's glove there is one more problem you must be aware of. Young infielders have a tendency when they are standing at their position or playing catch to squeeze the hand and glove unconsciously. This excessive squeezing action ruins the pocket of the glove. A crease forms in the pocket which will cause fielding problems for the young infielders. Teach your infielders to constantly pound the pockets of the glove as they play catch and before every pitch. Teach them how to form and preserve the deep and open face pocket. This will help minimize fielding errors.*

Coach, you should check every player's glove once a week. Make sure every week that the gloves are: (1) lubricated with shaving cream, NOT OIL, (2) fingers are tightly bonded, and (3) the pockets are formed and preserved properly.

THE INFIELDER

The fundamentals and techniques of each infield position will be covered by position. In this section, the information presented applies to all infielders. The commonalities of infield play that you must teach your infielders are as follows:

Anticipation

Fielding is ANTICIPATION, REACTION, and ADJUSTMENTS. Each ground ball in every game is a new experience for the novice and experienced player. As he fields he is adjusting to the game situation as he is making the play. Therefore, there is really no such thing as a "routine" play. Coach, you must teach the infielder how to "read" the ground ball, anticipate it's movement, and how to adjust and react to every new game situation. This is the essence of fielding.

Instincts

As a player learns to anticipate and adjust to every game situation he begins to think for himself. This developmental process is called *instinct or game awareness*. **This is a teachable skill.** If you constantly replicate game conditions in practice so a young infielder learns how to make quick decisions, anticipates and reacts positively in new game situations, you are teaching him game awareness---INSTINCTS. This is a critical skill that is often neglected because some coaches believe some players are "born" with natural instincts. These coaches believe that some players have natural instincts and some don't, so why bother teaching something that must come naturally. But, in fact, this belief is wrong.

DON'T JUST ANTICIPATE THE BALL WITH EVERY PITCH. BELIEVE THAT IT WILL BE SMOKED AT YOU EVERY PITCH (ALERTNESS).

All infielders must think "SIDE TO SIDE" until the ball is hit (develops quickness). IF HE LEANS FORWARD, HE WILL BE LATE TOO OFTEN.

The Ready Position

Teaching the young infielder to anticipate, and helping him develop his instincts, starts with teaching him the importance of being ready on every pitch. All infielders must develop a sense of looking for the ball---a desire to want the next grounder. Therefore, with every pitch, all infielders must be in the correct ready position.

The Stance for the Ready Position

- Comfortable and balanced---ready to move quickly.
- Relaxed.
- Body and glove up---quicker than if the body and glove are low, but if the novice infielder is afraid and won't stay down on a ground ball, then lower his ready position. If this doesn't work, remove him from the infield.
- Head up, feet approximately shoulder width and pointing outwardly, not straight ahead.
- Knees are bent, as the infielder is on the balls of his feet, not his toes.
- Arms are close to his body.
- As the ball is delivered, most infielders like to take one or two steps forward---not to be caught flat-footed or on their heels.
- First step to the ball that is to his side is a jab step with the leg and foot closest to the ground ball, then the cross-over step.
- If the ball is hit right at the infielder, if possible, "charge" the ball while under control.

<u>*READY POSITION*</u>   <u>*TRAPPING THE BALL*</u>

For young infielders this ready position
is okay. As the infielder gets older,
his glove and hand should be about knee
high for a quicker side step.

⓫ *COACHING TIP*

> *Coaches, stress that when the youngster fields the ground ball, you*
> *should see the infielder's chin down, his eyes looking the ball into the*
> *glove, and you should be able to see the button of his cap as he is*
> *bending over. As the ball enters the glove, the bare hand covers the*
> *ball while trapping it. Quickly, all in one motion, the feet shuffle to*
> *the proper throwing position with the hands buried into the chest*
> *lining up the directional side foot, knee, hip, shoulder and glove*
> *towards the target. This is one continuous movement that must be*
> *taught when fielding every ground ball.*

<u>Fielding Action</u>

Coach, you should teach this idea---fielding is a completed action. First,
fielding begins with trapping the ground ball in the glove, next shuffling
the body directionally to throw, and lastly, making the accurate throw.

<u>Accuracy</u>

Stress accuracy---reading the ground ball, trapping it, and making a good
throw.

Reactions

We have alluded to this important teachable skill. Reaction is simply first-step quickness. Coach, defensively, all players move to the ball in a variety of ways. Lateral movement, for example, is omnipresent all the time, all over the field. Therefore, in practice teach the players how to move side to side. When moving for any ball, first-step quickness is essential. Teach a player through reactionary drills to move quickly first with his feet then his body. The body always follows the feet. Stress to all players the importance of moving the feet first.

ⓑ *COACHING TIP*

> *As a youngster is learning how to field, it is important to teach him how to make the routine plays. But in reality, the routine play does not occur very often. Percentage wise, less than 50% of all ground balls are routine. Therefore, Coach, fungo many different kinds of grounders to your infielders.*

Communication

All infielders must communicate with each other and the outfielders before every pitch. Teach your infielders to anticipate what to do with every new hitter up and with men on base. Have a signal or cue that alerts all players what to do prior to each pitch---think as a unit.

Leadership

The shortstop is the captain of the infield. The catcher is the general. Defensively, these two vital players run the defense. Coach, identify these special players. Work with their exceptional talents. Develop their leadership qualities. Begin to give them developmental responsibilities. Build on this foundation, so eventually they will be able to run the defenses. They will become your "take charge" players as they lead by example.

The name of the game is BASEBALL, GRAB A BASE! Coach, during games young infielders have a tendency to stand around and watch the play develop. You must teach the young infielders when in doubt as to where to go and what to do---"grab" a base. Go to the nearest base and protect the bag.

Drills

- Jump rope.
- Ground ball development: (1) First, roll or hit slow rollers with the infielders using batting gloves (use soft baseballs then regular baseballs); and (2) as you increase speed and hardness of the balls, the infielders should use their regular small gloves.
- Daily fungo a variety of ground balls, beginning with the routine grounders and build on them. Stress accuracy and good mechanics in fielding and throwing.
- Pop up drills.
- Get dirty---teach all infielders to dive after reachable balls.

THE CATCHER

Emphasize to the young catcher, he is the key to a strong defense. He must learn how to take charge. Through positive affirmations, you can teach the youngster to be your field general. Give him the chance to succeed. Teach him how to call his own game and run your defenses.

Catching skills have eroded over the last twenty years with the advent of the "Johnny Bench one-handed catching style." Hall of Famer, Johnny Bench's receiving skills were extraordinary. His one-handed style was a trend setter. The problem is that the next generation of catchers did not possess Bench's motor abilities. Therefore, we advocate that all amateur coaches should teach their catchers to receive with two hands.

The two-handed catcher must use the old donut type glove. This glove will help the young catcher towards maximizing his performance potential: softer hands, relying more on his footwork, thus enhancing his receiving and throwing skills.

Calling Signals

The catcher should first signal the type of pitch, then give the location of the pitch.

The Receiving Position

After the catcher comes out of the sign-given stance, the catcher gets up into the ready position (jockey position) to receive the ball. To be able to throw, field a bunt or pop-up, he must have a stance which is not only comfortable, but one which he feels he can get out of quickly. As the catcher crouches down ready for the pitch, he must have a low stance and a low target. Stance characteristics are as follows:

- The glove hand is relaxed and not locked. The pitcher will not see a full pocket. He sees more or less the top half of the glove.
- The feet are no more than shoulder width apart. The toe of the right foot is about on the line with the heel of the left foot, and pointing toward first base.
- Your thighs and lower part of the legs form almost a right angle. Your weight is slightly forward on the balls of your feet. However, you don't lift the heels. You are up on the toe of the right foot, and the left foot is planted a little more solidly than the right one.
- Readiness---the catcher must have a feeling of readiness---ready to go or move. Young players do not anticipate early enough. Create anticipatory drills in practice. Always start from a balanced position.
- Receiving--the catcher, in receiving the pitch, should give slightly with his glove as the ball hits it, at the same time drawing the ball toward his belt buckle. Catching pitches with two hands give the receiver a chance to adjust the ball in his throwing hand while bringing the arm and glove back into the throwing position. THE CATCHER MUST GET INTO THE HABIT OF BEING READY TO THROW ON EVERY PITCH.
- The catcher can speed up his release time by placing his throwing hand behind or near the glove for a quicker exchange.
- Teach the young catcher a variety of throws. The old school of thought was to teach that the throw was made only from the shoulder, and not a complete sweep of the arm. This is not true anymore.
  - Try to get the ball off the best way you can.

- Have a cross-seam grip on the ball if possible.
- Variety of throws: (1) the full overhand throw, (2) the shoulder snap throw, and (3) the sidearm flip.
- It is important not to catch the ball flat-footed. You want to be on your toes and leaning toward the target-base. The crow-hop steps should be taught to young catchers because of the added body momentum needed to reach the ball to second base.

Handling the Low Pitch

The catcher's hands should be held out away from his body in a RELAXED fashion. He must not be rigid. He must handle pitches below the waist with the fingers pointing down. **The low pitch in the dirt must be stopped!** Teach the catcher to first automatically drop down to his knees, block the baseballs---don't try and catch them. As the catcher receives balls to the side and low in front of him, he should stick the foot out and slide keeping the shoulders square, chin down, body low, while keeping the ball between his legs. He must learn to drop down and keep the ball in front of him. Stress this important skill. Daily drills for this low pitch reaction are a must.

Tagging the Runner

Teach your catcher to tag all runners with two hands. A sweeping one-handed tag is used only as a last resort when there is a close play at the plate and the catcher has to reach for the runner.

Pop-Ups

All pop-ups should be caught with two hands. The pop-up comes down in a curving flight. Try and face the backstop when making the catch. On all in between pop-ups the first baseman and the third baseman have priority.

Fielding Bunts

Unless the ball is dead on the grass, (bare-handed) use two hands to field and pick up the moving ball.

Blocking the Plate

Catchers must show the plate to the incoming runner. Place one foot on the corner of the plate, revealing the plate, while forcing the runner to slide. Then the catcher brings his leg to the runner facing his knee at the runner and bracing his lower body while blocking the plate.

Hustle

Hustle for all foul balls. Usually, the pitcher wants the same ball back. Hustle down the first base line trailing the hitter with no runners on base. It looks good and maybe the hustling catcher might be in a position to back up a wild throw.

Studying the Hitters

Even young catchers can learn how to pitch to the opposing hitters.

Drills

- Daily---the catcher should block pitches in the dirt with two hands and the body down on both knees.
- Chalk talks---teach the catcher how to call a game.
- Throwing to each base (daily)---as the catcher receives pitches and throws, learn how to throw to a designated base, while constantly working on throwing mechanics and accuracy.
- Pop-up drills.

THE CATCHER

A. The Stance

B. Line Up to Target

C. The Throw

Ⓝ *COACHING TIP*

The first baseman and the third baseman should think of themselves as middle infielders. Think side-to-side.

THE FIRST BASEMAN

Coach, the first baseman is very important. Outside the catcher and the pitcher, he handles the baseball more than any other player. Therefore, his defensive skills are important to the whole team.

The Glove

The first baseman's glove can be a disadvantage. Teach the first baseman soft hands with a normal size glove, bare-handed drills, or use only batting gloves. Then move on to the larger first baseman's glove. Remember coach, if you are not careful, the larger first baseman's glove will do the work and not the young player's hand. This common fault leads to stiff hands and poor catching skills.

Soft Hands

Like any other infielder, he needs to work on his "soft hands." Fungo bare-handed grounders, batting glove grounders, and softball bare-hand ground balls to your first baseman.

Ground Balls

Like all infielders, the fielding position for ground balls is very important. All infielders must overcome fear of getting hit. Use softer balls before using the baseball to overcome this fear factor.

Getting to the Bag

The first instinct of the first baseman is to get to the bag as quickly as possible.

Footwork

If the player is right-handed, always receive every throw with the right foot on the base and vice-versa if the player is left-handed. The player should have both heels in contact with the bag while awaiting the throw.

Catching

Coach, stress to your first basemen that they should catch most throws with two hands.

Low Throws

The player must learn to "give" with the low throw. He has to pull his hands back into his body the moment the ball enters the glove, rather than let his hands and glove go out toward the ball.

Defensive Plays

Set up daily practices for the following plays: (1) all types of ground balls, (2) handling bunts, (3) throwing to second, third and home bases, (4) the unassisted put-out, (5) timing with the pitcher as he covers first base, (6) cutoffs and relays, (7) pop flies, and (8) pick-offs.

Drills

- Daily: Hit all types of ground balls and pop flies. Hit "betweener grounders" with pitcher covering first base. Throw low throw picks.
- Fungo grounders so that the first baseman has to make a variety of throws: double plays to second, bunts to third, relays to the catcher, and cutoffs to second base.

THE FIRST BASEMAN
(1) If right-handed, receive all throws
with right foot always on the bag.
(2) Whenever possible, stretch with two
hands.

THE THIRD BASEMAN

The "hot corner." This is the best description of third base. There is always action at this base. Prepare him for the following:

Instincts

The third baseman needs game awareness instincts. He must always be "alive" during the game. He must be ready for the hot smashes, slow rollers or bunts, and sliding base runners.

The Glove

Use a small hand size glove with a well formed pocket. Develop "soft hands" (see First Baseman).

A Variety of Throws

The third baseman needs to learn all the different kinds of throws that are required of him at this position.

Playing the Hitters

Just like all the other infielders, he needs to learn how to play the opposing hitters.

Making the Double Play

Teach him how to throw to second to initiate the double play and tag his own base to start his double play.

Bunt Situations

Teach him how to field bunts.

Plays at Third

Teach the third baseman how to tag a runner, lineup and set-up the cutoffs from the left fielder, how to cover the bag in different base running situations, handle run-down plays, pick-offs, and catching pop flies.

Drills

- Reactionary drills: Fungo line drives and hard smash ground balls.
- Fungo a variety of ground balls, bunts and pop flies.
- Throws: he must learn a variety of throws to all the bases and learn how to throw off-balance.

THE THIRD BASEMAN
(1) Think: Every hit will be smoked at me.
(2) Be prepared; third base is a side-to-side position.

THE SECOND BASEMAN

All infielders must develop quick feet and hands. Remember, you throw first with your feet then your hands. Stress getting rid of the ball as quickly as possible. When playing catch, all infielders must catch and throw all in one motion using the shuffle crow-hop throw. Develop "soft hands" (see First Baseman).

The second baseman must learn a variety of throws. Therefore, in practice hit a great volume of different kinds of ground balls.

The Pivot

Young second basemen should learn as soon as possible how to make the double play. The double play is a difficult play to master because of the different kinds of throws the second baseman makes and receives, and having to avoid the sliding base runner. Therefore, all second basemen are required to learn a variety of pivots. Find out which pivot is most comfortable for the youngster and allow him to use his choice pivot. Later on he will learn all five pivots. DON'T BE A JACK OF ALL TRADES AND MASTER OF NONE!

The Glove

Use a small hand size glove.

Drills

- Daily: Fungo a variety of ground balls, pop flies, and double plays with a shortstop and third baseman.
- Throws: Daily, he must make a variety of throws to first, second and third bases, and throws for relays and cutoffs.

THE SHORTSTOP

Again, **the shortstop is the captain of the infield.** He must have peripheral vision, game awareness and instincts. He may lack quickness or range, but if he is your best fielder and has the most accurate arm, then develop his leadership and game instinct qualities. If the shortstop possesses leadership and game instincts, he will more than make-up for any motor skill he may lack at this position.

The Glove

Use a small hand size glove. Develop "soft hands" (see First Baseman).

Playing the Hitters

Teach your young shortstop how to "play" the hitters---remember the opposing hitter's running speed and his hitting tendencies. Also, the shortstop should know his own strengths and weaknesses.

The Double Play

Coach, teach the young shortstop the following **Double Play Fundamentals:**

Getting to the Base

Arrive early and with balance, cheat toward second before the pitch, slow down as you approach the bag by using short choppy steps to get balanced.

The Pivot

There are a variety of pivots used by the shortstop depending on the type of throw he receives from the second and first basemen. Teach the youngster to come across the base to the right side (right field side) and drag the corner of the base with his right foot as he glides across the base. This pivot is the most common and easiest to learn.

Tagging the Runner

The safest way to tag the runner is the stationary tag. As the shortstop straddles the bag, he places his glove on the ground in front of the bag and lets the runner slide into it. Closing the thumb over the glove, he lets the runner slide into the back of the glove.

Receiving the Catcher's Throw

The young shortstop must get to the bag as quickly as possible to set up properly for the throw. He must "cheat" closer to the base on steal situations. In making the tag, the shortstop should have the back of the bag hooked under his left foot so he can be under better control. As he receives the throw, both knees are quickly bent to get the glove down close to the ground. The glove is placed in front of the base with the back of the glove making contact with the runner. As the runner makes contact with the glove, the shortstop pulls his glove out and away in a sweeping motion. Remember, teach the shortstop never to expose the baseball to the sliding runner.

Signs

As the captain of the infield, the shortstop should give the following signs: (1) to the pitcher, second baseman and to the outfield when he initiates pick-offs; (2) to the pitcher and second baseman---who will be covering the bag on come backers to the pitcher and throws from the catcher; and (3) to the outfield, when he wants to move the outfielders.

Pick-Off Plays

Daily or weekly practice learning pick-off plays is important for young infielders so they can develop the necessary timing of these plays. Coach, the primary purpose of pick-off plays is not to pick-off a lot of runners, but to keep the runners close to the base.

Drills

- Leadership: Constantly work with the shortstop as he develops leadership qualities through private one-on-one meetings and chalk talks.
- Cutoffs: Teach him how to position himself for the cutoff---how to receive the throw and quickly throw to the right base (throw and turn) to glove side.
- Fungo a variety of ground balls and fly balls to the shortstop.
- Double plays: The shortstop must learn to work with the second baseman for the right timing and mechanics of the double play.

THE OUTFIELDER

In youth leagues, most coaches do not give the attention to the outfielders that they give the infielders. Most coaches put all their best players into the infield. As a consequence, the outfielders are sometimes treated as second class citizens. Their self-esteem has been wounded.

Self Esteem

Coach, you must convince the outfielders that they are important to your defense. They are essential to your team effort. Therefore, make them feel wanted and needed.

Leadership

Your center fielder is the leader of your outfield. Work with him to develop leadership qualities.

Communication

All the outfielders must learn to work together as a unit. This concept will instill importance in their jobs and raise their levels of self-esteem.

Communication begins in practice. They must help each other when judging fly balls, backing each other up, and helping each other to throw to the right base or cutoff man.

The Glove

A long-fingered glove with considerable webbing and a deep pocket.

The Stance

The outfielder should use a comfortable stance. He semi-crouches, with his hands in front of his knees. He is set, but not tense, and always alert. As the pitch is delivered, he follows it towards the plate, stays on the balls of his feet, ready to pivot and crossover in either direction.

The Throw

Teach all outfielders to throw over the top with a long route releasing the ball with 12-6 rotation. Every throw should be made with quick crow-hop feet. Teach the outfielder to "hit" the cutoff man whenever possible.

Judging the Fly

Judging the fly ball is the single most important skill of the outfielder. All daily practices must have judging fly ball drills. Teach youngsters to catch the fly ball with two hands while moving in towards the infield. Get rid of one-handed fielding.

Rule of Thumb

If the ball is hit at them and over their heads, the outfielder should turn to his glove side (left if right-handed) and go back on the ball. The outfielder must turn and run back, not backpedaling. As your outfielders improve going back on the fly ball, you can progressively teach the advanced outfielder to run while not looking at the ball. He will learn to turn for the ball when and where he thinks it is coming down.

Fielding grounders

Outfielders should field like an infielder; use two hands, stay low to the ground, look the ball into the glove, if they are having trouble fielding you could have them go down on one knee.

Playing the Hitters

Outfielders, like infielders, must learn where to play each opposing hitter. Coach, help your outfielders learn how to play the hitters. You can use the shortstop to help move the outfielders.

Fear of Fence

As the ball is hit, the outfielder should turn and run as fast as he can to the fence. Once at the fence, he is ready for the catch, even if he has to come back five feet to catch it. Don't backpedal to the fence. Get to the fence in a hurry and then place one hand on the fence for possible "whereabouts" information.

Drills

- Fungo "gappers" between two outfielders. They will learn to communicate together.
- Fungo a variety of hits: off fences, into corners, line drives, high flies into the sun and at night, and grounders of all kinds. In other words, hit fungoes that will simulate batted game hits.
- During batting practice have your outfielders practice getting "jumps" and ground balls off the batted baseballs.

THE OUTFIELDER

BOX SCORE

Good players are not born, they are developed.
How?...Inform, Instruct and Inspire.

Plan developmental practices and drills. Planned
preparation is a function of smart coaching.

V
Running

"We all can run, but only a few can 'motor'."

--Dr. Coop DeRenne

Baseball is a quick and a ballistic sport. Throwing, swinging a bat and sprinting require ballistic movements. For a hundred years we have been training baseball players as if they were long distance track athletes. This aerobic training is wrong. Baseball is an anaerobic sport, therefore, you must teach our young players how to run and sprint. You must understand that everyone's body type is different. Do not try to fit every one in the same mold. Realizing this point, there are still some basic running fundamentals that will apply to all sprinters.

The Chicago White Sox' SCHOOL OF THIEVES: Chicago has a "Running Fraternity" called the School of Thieves. Throughout the whole organization, the players with the most base running and base stealing potential are members of this elite club. In Spring Training, these runners were brought into camp three days early with the pitchers and catchers.

During these three days, the intense "school of thievery" was held. The White Sox' base running staff of instructors worked with these speedsters to improve their base running and base stealing skills. A base running coordinator throughout the season will follow-up these Spring Training sessions by visiting all six minor league teams and continue to work with these elite runners. Some of the main points stressed in the School of Thieves are as follows:

- *Warm-up*

  15-20 minutes, general warm-up---stretching, light jogging. Specific warm-up---sit downs of pumping arm actions, high bounding runs, first-two step steals, 30 yard sprints from base stealing stance, and backward runs (stretching hamstrings).

- *Good base stealing mechanics*

  Lead off (approximately 7 feet): Balance body on the balls of the feet, semi-crouched with arms relaxed hanging down thigh high (not on the knees); eyes glued on the pitcher.

  Feet: The right toes are in line with the instep of the left foot and turned slightly out.

  Arms: Pumping arms come naturally into the body. One arm probably will come across the body more than the other. Do not turn the shoulders.

  Balance: Keep the athlete in balance by pumping the arms so that the hands do not go any higher than just below the chin.

  Action/Reaction: The arms and legs move in action/reaction manner. As the left arm comes up, the right leg comes up, while simultaneously the right arm goes back past the hip. The vise-versa: as the right arm comes up, the left leg comes up, while simultaneously the left arm goes back past the hip.

The first two steps are the key, the first step has two movements.

- *First Movement:* THE FIRST MOVEMENT GETS YOU INTO THE RUNNING POSITION. This first movement is a PIVOT as the runner tries to be moving a little, creating a stimulus. The right arm pulls in tight as the left arm turns and comes across the body, helping the hips rotate and pivot the feet. PIVOT AND DRIVE! The results of the pivot produce the right leg and left arm forward and the right arm and left leg back. The body is leaning forward over the right leg on the balls of its feet toward second base. Stay low, keeping the hands shoulder height, so you will not raise up.

- *Second Movement:* The second movement is the cross-over step. As the body and feet pivot, the left leg crosses over the right leg. It is very important that as the left leg crosses over the right leg, the right arm reacts and pumps forward. The left arm goes back to the left hip quickly to continue the pumping action as the right leg provides the base for the drive forward.

The Second Step: The second step is a continuation of the first step. After the cross-over, the body must stay low and lean forward as the feet and arms accelerate the body. With this step, the body is beginning to accelerate into good running technique.

Ⓜ *COACHING TIP*

Coach, have all your young athletes practice the above running mechanics in practice every day. Have them begin learning these mechanics by "walking" them through the fundamentals slowly, then gradually picking up the pace. Eventually, the players will master the arm and leg lifts at a full running in place speed. Then they are ready for sprint work.

FIRST TWO-STEP
TAKEOFF

The Stance   *The Pivot*   *The Cross-Over*

- ## *Get Out of Batter's Box*

(1) Site first base early and run through the bag, do not lunge for the bag; (2) always run pumping arms as fast as possible while under control, so that the hands come up to chin level; (3) think double out of box and round first base hard, anticipating the error while looking to take the extra base; (4) round first base hitting the inside corner of bag with either foot; (5) when rounding first base, drop the left shoulder and lean toward second; (6) when rounding the bag, pick up the outfielder and ball as your opposite arm and leg work together to slow down, or see an error and quickly shuffle and accelerate for the extra base.

Out of the Batter's Box   *Rounding First Base*

• *Pickle*

If you get picked off first base, you should get into a run down and try and bring the shortstop and second baseman close together. Hopefully, this action will cause a bad throw, maybe you will be able to run by one of them as he is trying to tag you. **NEVER GET CAUGHT STANDING STILL.**

• *First Base Lead-Offs*

(1) Keep body low and leaning toward second; (2) step-back lead--- this is a safe lead-off distance that you can step back; first take one step with left foot then a right cross-over step onto the bag and swing yourself around and face the infield; (3) walking lead-off; (4) two-way lead-off---shuffle out and fix your feet knowing the distance off first base without looking at the ground; at this distance you can go to either base.

Lead-Off

🎾 *COACHING TIP*

On every lead-off the goal is to get yourself moving toward the next base. If you get movement, then you will have a good jump and should increase your percentage of stolen bases. The rule is: get MOVEMENT, then go!

- *Reading the Pitcher*

  - *Right-handers:* (1) the head is deceiving, it is used to hold runners; (2) pitchers will vary their tempos---be cautious and shuffle a little to get more distance; (3) when shuffling, if the pitcher throws over, always DIVE BACK; (4) focus on: left shoulder turn, hand and glove break, lifting of right planted heel, quick arm or feet action, slow arm or feet action.

  - *Left-handers:* (1) head is deceiving---some give one look or two looks, some look home then throw to first and vise versa; (2) high kickers---go! (3) look for balk move, stepping over the 45 degree line, or if his foot comes past the rubber; (4) steal on first movement by the pitcher (gambling).

  - *Lead-off:* Lead off when the pitcher is getting his sign. He can't look at you and the catcher at the same time. Try and get maximum lead-off and fix your feet while he is getting into his stretch position. If you have movement and he does not stop you, then steal the base---ACTIVE BASE STEALING, NOT PASSIVE!

- *Second Base*

  (1) Always take three shuffles toward third, if he doesn't stop you, go; (2) **NEVER TAKE YOUR EYES OFF THE PITCHER,** the third base coach will watch the second baseman and the shortstop; (3) take three shuffles---time them so that when the pitcher turns and goes to the plate you take off for third, or if he throws back to second on your last shuffle you plant the right foot and hustle back to second; (4) shuffle out on the balls of your feet, not on your toes.

- *Third Base*

  (1) Sprint home on a ground ball by being alert to the ball-bat contact; (2) always have shoulders square to the plate ready to break for the plate; (3) watch the pitch and if you see curveball spin or a very low pitch, anticipate a dirt ball and shuffle out extra to see if the

ball gets away from catcher far enough for you to go home; (4) if caught in a run-down (pickle) sprint back and forth as fast as possible trying to draw more than two throws; (5) stealing of home---look at the catcher and notice how he is setting up, try and pick an off-speed pitch or curveball to go on, if you get movement and the pitcher doesn't stop you or see you, then go.

- *Base Running*

ALERTNESS is the key to good base running. Speed is secondary. Good base running is a function of ALERTNESS, SPEED, and SLIDING ABILITY.

Alertness Rules

- Again, on any hit to the outfield, think double. Round first base hard looking for the error or extra base. A misplayed ball that kicks away from the outfielder and directionally from the throwing base is a signal to take the extra base (**ANTICIPATE!**).

- Anticipate the poor throw by a position player especially the outfielder. If the throw is off-target or too high from the outfielder coming in toward the infield, take the extra base.

- When leading off from first base and second base, shuffle (3 shuffles) out and lean toward the next base as the ball is crossing the plate, anticipating a passed ball. If the pitch is a curve ball, anticipate it will be in the dirt, hard to handle by the catcher, always looking for the passe ball to advance to the next base.

- When running the bases, have peripheral vision. Look ahead and over your shoulder for the misplayed error. If the outfielder is catching the ball as he is back pedalling (can't get off a strong and accurate throw) take the extra base. Challenge the outfielders.

- When leading off from third base anticipate a passed ball with every pitch. Be cautious, but be alert.

Second Base Tag-Up

Third Base Tag-Up

- <u>*Sliding*</u>

Sliding is really a controlled fall. It is not a leap. The key element to a good slide is timing. The slide must not begin too soon or too late. **Never change your mind.**

First, teach the bent-leg slide. This is the safest and fastest slide into the base. It also allows the base runner to pop up quickly and to be ready to advance to the next base. The mechanics of the bent-leg slide with the pop up are as follows:

- Begin the slide about seven feet from the base.
- Take off from either leg and bend it under the other leg.
- Slide on the calf of the bottom bent leg.
- As you go into the slide, sit down and automatically you will put the bottom leg underneath.
- Keep low to the ground. Do not jump or leap for the base.
- As you slide, throw your head back and arms into the air, preventing the knees from hitting the ground first.
- Turn the instep of the bottom foot in the direction of the slide, prevent the spikes from catching in the ground.
- Tag the base with the top leg which is relaxed, loose and well off the ground.
- Keep the top leg slightly bent and the heel off the ground.
- Ride the calf of the bottom leg into the base.
- As the runner contacts the base, he should brace the bent leg.
- The runner then rolls inward on his bottom knee, rising to an upright position. With the aid of the speed of his slide, the runner will be ready to advance to the next base.

The Hook Slide

The hook slide is used by the runner to avoid being tagged by the infielder. Coach, you must understand that when the base runner hook slides and reaches out with that foot and tries to catch the base with his toe, he is sliding 93 (3 extra feet) feet to get to the base. This can be a disadvantage, as well as a deception advantage. The key to the hook slide is to keep the touching foot straight until the runner hits the base.

Head-First Slide

There is controversy over which slide is the fastest, feet-first of head-first. The head-first slide is definitely more dangerous. We recommend teaching the young player to use the bent-leg, feet-first slide for injury prevention and base running alertness.

Sliding Drills

- Practice with football pants, tennis shoes, and clench your hands loosely in the air when sliding.
- Practice in a sand sliding pit.
- Practice on wet grass or wet plastic-grass runways.
- The inexperienced slider should start sliding at shorter distances.

The Bent Knee
"Pop-Up" Slide

The Hook Slide

- *Additional Base Stealing Tips*

Attitude

Young base stealers must develop an attitude of aggressiveness and confidence. The high success-failure ratio breeds **confidence**. Therefore, coach, create a high success-attempt ratio by teaching intelligent base stealing. You can not have a fear of failure. When Rickey Henderson broke the single-season base stealing record in 1982, he also set the record for "caught stealings." **With information and awareness comes confidence.**

Coach, help the base stealers gather knowledge from the pitcher and catcher, and help them get good leads. When they will feel they are better than the pitchers and catchers, all fears of failure will be eliminated. They will become aggressive and rise to the challenge. Also, **you should always get your base stealers "back in the saddle" after failure or when they are in a slump.** When they are in a slump, do the following:

- Work with their lead offs.
- Review their first-two step quickness acceleration starts.
- Help them to study the pitcher's moves more closely.
- You select a high percentage pitch or situation for them to steal.
- Show confidence in them---keep sending them. They must learn to be daring, take chances, and eliminate fear of failing.

Know the count: Depending on the count, pitchers have tendencies. Steal on the breaking pitch or change-up whenever possible.

Pitchers Characteristics: Again, study the pitcher's pick-off moves and his quick or slow delivery to the plate. Coach, keep an opposing pitcher's log on every pitcher in your league:

- Type of pitcher.
- Pitch selection tendencies.
- Type of delivery to the plate.
- Type of pick off moves, etc.

⚾ *COACHING TIP*

Keys to Stealing:

- *Movement.*
- *Distance.*
- *See action of pitcher toward the plate.*

BOX SCORE

You can't make a plow horse into a thoroughbred. You can develop all horses into race contenders...INFORM, INSTRUCT AND INSPIRE.

VI
Pitching Mechanics

*"You get hitters out two ways: location or change of speed.
If you can't locate, you must change speeds.
If you can't change speeds, you must locate.
If you can't do either, become an accountant."*

--Tom House

High-tech equipment and recent research have combined together to provide state-of-the-art information and techniques about pitching mechanics. No longer do we have to rely on pitching coaches' opinions and/or intuitive reasoning.

The pitching mechanics presented here were discovered through research methodologies and motion analysis technology. American league pitchers' game performances were analyzed from 1986 to 1991 using Bio-Kinetics' Computerized Motional Analysis System. This company's major league pitching and hitting databases are the most extensive and accurate in the world. From the collected data we have determined the pitching and hitting absolutes that all successful major league pitchers and hitters have in common. Based on these absolutes and commonalities, the "ideal" pitching and hitting models have been developed.

Please read, review, and re-read this chapter so that you have a good mental image and understanding of the vocabulary and concepts. Understanding this chapter is critical for player development, performance, and injury prevention.

THE DELIVERY

There are 14 sequences in the pitching delivery. No matter how different pitchers' body types vary or their own individual styles differ (e.g. windup or no windup) all deliveries have a 14 step-by-step sequence. One complete delivery begins with the starting stance and ends with the follow-through.

This 14 sequence evolution is supported by the data collected and analyzed by Bio-Kinetics, Inc. a "think-tank" in Laguna Hills, California. Using their high-speed cameras and computerized motion analysis system, the 14 components in the delivery are based on Newton's Laws of Motion. The results reveal that the 14 delivery components are contained within four motion absolutes. These four absolutes are: **BALANCE, DIRECTION, LAUNCH/DECEPTION, and WEIGHT TRANSFER.**

As we proceed through the delivery from stance to follow-through these four absolutes will be present. Therefore, the interrelationship of the 14 delivery components and the four absolutes work in tandem as a ballet of movement. This interrelation process is called INTEGRATION. As you will notice as we go through the delivery, all pitching deliveries consist of two movements: **linear (or straight forward movement) and angular (or rotational movement), both working together in tandem.** Again, as we proceed through the delivery, we will point out the linear and angular relationship.

🔘 *COACHING TIP*

Coach, we can't overemphasize that you must understand the importance of this relationship of the pitcher's linear and rotational movements through his delivery. Again, as the pitcher winds up and proceeds through all 14 components and the four absolutes, his total body moves through two sequential movements---linear, then rotational. If the pitcher intermixes his linear and rotational movements, then he is subject to mechanical problems and increases the possibility of a serious arm injury.

THE DELIVERY COMPONENTS

The Starting Stance

The starting stance from the wind-up position should include the following:

- Eyes on target.

- Your weight should be evenly distributed with the pivot foot half on and half in front of the rubber. Keep a balanced stance.

- Always hide the ball. Don't find your grip until your hands come together, then keep the back of the glove up and toward the hitter with ball, fingers, and wrist deep in the pocket of the glove.

- Right-handed pitchers (RHP) should work from the right side of the rubber, left-handed pitchers (LHP) from the left side. Do not sacrifice comfort on the rubber, but if you have no foot position preference, try this method.

Initiating the Wind-Up

Initiating the wind-up correctly should include the following:

- If you are right-handed, start on the right side of the rubber and vice versa. Transfer some weight to back foot with a small reverse or side step, leaving the button of your cap over the pivot foot while comfortably lifting your hands as high as you desire. We recommend young pitchers bring their hands together and bury them into their chest area. Find the grip on the ball, making sure the ball is well hidden in the glove.

- When the glove reaches its highest point, place the pivot foot down in front of rubber (not on top and not half on/half off), but down in front to set the beginning for a firm "posting" with the pivot leg.

- Keep the head, or the button of cap over the pivot foot at all times.

    NOTE: THE BACK FOOT WILL BECOME PART OF THE PITCHER'S FRONT OR DIRECTIONAL SIDE AS HIS DELIVERY CONTINUES.

The Pivot Position

A good pivot position will include:

- Transfer your weight from the back foot to the posting foot.

- The back leg begins movement directly to the plate, becoming part of the directional or front side.

- Keep the head forward of the shoulders with the chin tucked slightly toward the front shoulder on a route directly in line with home plate.

  NOTE: THROWING FROM THE STRETCH POSITION IS THE SAME MECHANICALLY ONCE THE PITCHER HAS TRANSFERRED HIS WEIGHT TO THE POSTING FOOT.

The Start Forward

When starting forward, a pitcher should do the following:

- The hands and front leg start toward a natural "closing off" or "tuck" position at the same time.

- The shoulders start to line up directly with home plate.

- The head stays forward of the shoulders with the chin staying close to the front shoulder.

- Start the front knee toward the belt buckle by **LIFTING** with the thigh muscles. DO NOT KICK OR SWING this leg at any time---it causes the upper body to compensate by leaning back, forcing it off the direct line toward home plate. This movement is called a **"quad lift."**

The Post Position (Attaining Balance)

The post position is important to good throwing mechanics and should include the following:

- You should move from the quad lift into a solid posting on the strong side with the button of pitcher's cap over the ball of your post foot. Do not collapse or rock off this post position by bending the post leg excessively. Do not lean back from this position with the upper body; keep the shoulders in line with home plate.

- Close off the front or directional side to a **"beat"** (wait 1 second) of balance. Let the shoulder, hip, and leg close together, like a gate, at an angle that is natural and comfortable---usually to a point over the rubber.

- **Do not start forward with your delivery until the front knee reaches its highest point of elevation.** Height of the knee and length of arm arc are directly related---a pitcher with a high leg kick usually takes a long arc with throwing arm and vice versa. Adjustments to hold runners close from the stretch position can be made after mechanics have been mastered (first absolute---BALANCE).

- **Try and keep your hands together and as close to the chest as possible until the body starts forward.** This will prevent the front side from flying open and sets the stage for the throwing hand and glove to separate in an action that promotes good direction.

Initiating the Delivery

Here's what should happen when the delivery begins:

- After the beat of balance (1 second) and the closing off of the front or directional side, **BEGIN A CONTROLLED FALL, NOT A VIOLENT PUSH OR DRIVE,** when striding toward home plate.

- The whole front or directional side takes a firm route toward home plate in a straight line between the pitcher's front shoulder and the catcher's face mask (second absolute---DIRECTION).

- Hands break naturally with gravity, TURNING THUMBS UNDERNEATH to force elbows up.

- The path of arm is unique to each pitcher within these parameters: with throwing arm, wrist stays on top of ball until arm begins forward acceleration. Fingers stay on top throughout delivery on all pitches. Arm swings naturally from shoulder when arm begins its arc on the back side. Front side arm, extended or bent, must stay directly on line with the throwing arm until the front foot lands and the throwing arm pushes it out of the way.

The Forward Stride

The following things can help you when taking a forward stride to the plate:

- Continue a controlled fall with the front foot leading the whole directional side toward home plate.

- The ball swings down, back, and up with the back of the wrist to the sky until throwing elbow approaches shoulder height. Concurrently, the front side elbow is approaching shoulder height in its route.

- The whole front side---shoulders, elbow, forearm, hip, leg and foot--- follow a direct route to home plate (**second absolute---DIRECTION**, linear body movement) to prepare for the foot landing and eventual weight transfer.

- Eyes center on target right over the top of front elbow and glove.

- The front side elbow and shoulder are as high and level with back side elbow and shoulder. As the front arm moves toward the target, the elbow and glove are "thrown" into the face of the hitter hiding the ball for deception purposes (**third absolute---DECEPTION**). This is called the "goalpost position."

Landing the Stride Foot

As the stride foot lands:

- The ball reaches its highest point in the arc of the arm on pitcher's strong side---ELBOW HEIGHT IS EVEN WITH SHOULDERS. Front side elbow is also shoulder height, setting the stage for an efficient wheeling motion.

- The pivot foot remains in contact with the rubber.

- The stride foot lands on a direct line with the target with the front knee, hip, shoulder, and elbow following in succession.

- The shoulders should be as close to level as possible with head slightly forward of body's midpoint and the chin buried against the front shoulder.

- Try to keep your head as low to the ground as possible as the stride foot lands.

- Length of the stride should not inhibit weight transfer.

Arm Acceleration

The following points are critical as the arm accelerates to throw the ball:

- **The throwing elbow and the front side elbow stays level with the shoulders.**

- The pivot foot leaves the rubber, and the weight is transferred to a bending stride leg.

- The strong (back) side begins replacing the directional side (enroute) to home plate.

- The directional side elbow should remain at least as high as the right or strong side elbow and on line directly toward the target until the weight transfer occurs and the action/reaction of throwing begins.

The Forward Thrust

With the arm thrusting forward correctly to release the ball, the following things occur:

- The throwing elbow leads the throwing arm forward. Throwing is internal rotation of shoulder and elbow.

- The strong side completely replaces the directional side as weight is transferred completely to the landing leg (fourth absolute---WEIGHT TRANSFER). At this point, the shoulders pass each other in opposite directions with head becoming an axis for the arm's path over a bent knee. Rotational movement initiated by the hips replaces linear movement.

- Glove hand and arm are pulled toward the body at exactly the same angle as the throwing arm comes through its arc---like a "captain's wheel."

- Problem Areas:
  - A "late" throwing arm is due to rushing through the balance point, causing the front foot to hit prematurely.
  - "Flying open" is due to using the front side as a power movement.
  - A dropped elbow position results from improper "posting" over strong back side (e.g. hands away from body, "kicking" the lift leg), or an abbreviated long figure eight arm route.

Releasing the Ball

Ball Release With Pronation
(Weight Over Landing Leg)

When the ball is released properly, the following should occur:

- The head is directly over the leverage leg.

- The arm snaps to full extension.

- The wrist is straight and firm behind the ball.

- The fingers are on top of ball---on all pitches. The grip on the ball is important because it affects rotation. Imparting rotation makes the ball move. Not everyone can throw the ball hard, but everyone can be taught to make the ball move.

Pronation of the Arm

When following things occur at point of the release and right after ball leaves fingertips of throwing arm:

- The throwing arm snaps straight to full extension at release point.

- The throwing arm pronates---the palm rotates thumb down and out, away from body---as the ball leaves the fingertips. This occurs on all pitches, breaking balls included.

- Weight begins to transfer forward of leverage knee---upper body is actually pulled through by the throwing arm. Keep the head low to the ground.

- The pivot heel continues to rotate out and up, as the foot begins to leave the rubber.

Weight Over the Leverage Leg---Weight Transfer

The following actions center the weight of a pitcher's body over the leverage leg:

- The shoulders, arms, and upper body extend and pivot around the axis created by pitcher's head over his leverage leg.

- The back leg comes off the rubber to counterbalance the upper body extension toward home plate.

- The more extension (**"bury nose into the target"**) a pitcher gets after releasing the ball, the better his upper body and legs absorb and dissipate the shock of throwing.

- Balance over landing leg is only important until the arm has decelerated.

The Follow-Through

The following things occur in a pitcher's follow-through:

- The throwing shoulder has driven toward the target, completing replacement of directional side with strong back side.

- The arm pronates and begins decelerating. The deceleration route of the throwing arm is across the body, down and lower than leverage leg's knee, ending up back past leverage leg's hip close to the ground (**"pickup dirt"**).

- The upper torso extends to absorb shock and helps the arm to slow down.

- The back side leg lifts off the rubber to balance the process.
  - Most sore or hurt posterior shoulders occur during the deceleration of the arm.
  - The better the balance from the back side leg, the more extension is achieved, and the better the upper body can absorb and distribute the shock of the throwing arm slowing down.

- Get the whole body under control and become an infielder with defensive responsibilities.

The Delivery Cues

The whole delivery can be taught through the following cueing phrase:

Bury → Pivot & Lift → Glove → Ball → Nose & Dirt

⚾ *COACHING TIP*

Coach, if you instruct young pitchers to remember the above cueing phrase as they begin learning their deliveries, they will automatically duplicate good pitching mechanics. If you try to teach them all 14 components in order and their relationship with the four absolutes, you will clutter their minds with confusing information. Frustration will set in.

TEACHING NOTE

Teach the young pitcher NOT TO WINDUP with his arms going overhead as he goes into his pivot position. If you teach him a no "wind-up" delivery, his hands will automatically come together into the chest area as he pivots which will help him get into the buried position. This buried position is so vital to the post-balanced position and to the separating of the hands with the thumbs underneath when he takes his ball route.

DELIVERY CUES

Stance

Pivot

Balance & Bury

Take

Replace

Dirt

PITCH GRIP MECHANICS

Your grip on a baseball is the final factor in your implementation of a quality pitch. Being efficient, effective, and putting rotation on the ball at the release point requires an overall command of body mechanics: good balance, proper direction, adequate weight transfer, and positive deception.

It is imperative that for good ball rotation or a "tight spin," the front (or directional) elbow and the throwing elbow must be on line with the target and at least shoulder height, as the front foot plants and the throwing arm accelerates to deliver the ball. Assuming that elbows are in the correct position throughout the delivery, there are some other absolutes which effect grip and rotation on the ball:

- The throwing arm rotates internally as it accelerates. It snaps perfectly straight at release and pronates inward during deceleration on all pitches.
- The arm position from elbow to shoulder is the same on every pitch, no matter what the pitch is. It is the arm position from elbow to finger tips which accounts for the spin on the ball. **Therefore, the spin that makes the ball move is a function of FOREARM/WRIST POSITION and proper FINGER PLACEMENT over the top of the ball at the release.**
- **The grip from which all pitches key is a cross-seam fastball grip.** This is a maximum velocity, maximum force pitch requiring that the total body stay behind the ball with forearm, wrist, and finger tips (especially the middle finger) imparting rotation directly through the middle of the ball. The palm of the hand is facing directly at the target at the release point. The ball, using the face of a clock for reference, would have a reverse "12 to 6" spin.
- To make the ball cut, slide, or curve requires increasing degrees of supination by forearm and wrist (supination means accelerating the forearm and wrist in a **"karate chop"** like action with the palm facing inward, toward the body). At the release point, the finger tips of your index and especially the middle finger are to the right (right-handed pitcher) of the center of the ball. The more supination, the further from the center the middle finger is, the more spin is generated over the upper right part of the ball as it is released.

Ideally, arm speed is the same as with a fast ball. The force of the finger tips on the ball is directed off of center, or over, instead of through the ball. The seams should have a forward "11 to 5" spin.

⑪ *COACHING TIP*

A final word on the curveball. Master it when the league allows the pitchers to throw it, not before. It is a more difficult pitch to hit than the slider. Remember, even in the big leagues, there are curveball hitters, but nobody hits a good curveball. We have never seen a losing pitcher who could throw a curveball for strikes. we believe the curveball should be taught only to high school pitchers.

The Curveball

- To make the ball run, sink, or screw requires increasing degrees of pronation by the forearm and wrist. (Pronation means accelerating the wrist and forearm with the palm facing out, away from the body, leading with the thumb side of the hand.) At the release point, the finger tips of the index and especially the middle finger are on top of, but to the left of center of the ball. The more pronation, the further from center the middle finger gets and the more spin is generated over the upper region of the ball as it is released. Ideally, arm speed is the same as with a fastball. The force of the finger tips on the ball is directed off of center, or over, instead of through the ball. The seams should have a forward, "1 to 7" spin.

- A change-up is a pitch that is gripped to minimize the force exerted by the finger tips on the ball at the release point, while still maintaining arm speed. There are numerous grips---from splitting the fingers to "choking" the ball back in the hand. **Final choice for a change grip is a function of comfort, feel, and command.** Any grip that maintains arm speed and minimizes the force (therefore the velocity) imparted to the ball at release will work. An average major league pitcher has the most success if his change-up is 17-22 mph slower than his best fastball.

- Finally, there is only 1/4" difference in finger placement over the top of the ball between the biggest curveball and the biggest screwball, theoretically the two extremes of a pitcher's movement/action repertoire. Velocity always decreases as the middle finger is moved away from the center of the ball. **There is no true grip for any pitch---it is a function of hand size and comfort.** The grips shown here are only starting points. These are traditional finger placements on seams to show you the basics so that you can determine what works best for you.

Fastball

Change-Up

Curveball

PITCHING THOUGHTS
BY
CY YOUNG WINNER
BRET SABERHAGEN

In January, 1990, Bret Saberhagen and four other big league players and coaches gave a baseball clinic to Hawaii's local youth players and coaches. The following are some thoughts and pitching tips from two-time Cy Young winner and good friend, Bret Saberhagen...

SPRING TRAINING

"The first week of Spring Training is basically for conditioning. I do not throw too much. I play a lot of short/long toss and run sprints. I do not throw to a catcher. The next two weeks I throw to a catcher, but no curveballs. I only throw fastballs and change-ups. After the fourth week, I begin to throw my curveball. I really believe a big league pitcher must have a minimum of three pitches to be successful at this level. I am tested for arm strength on the Cybex machine. I also ride the LifeCycle stationary bike during Spring Training and during the season."

LEG WORK

"During Spring Training I run a lot of sprints to get my legs in shape. These sprints usually are foul line to foul line. You sprint one foul line to the other foul line and then walk back. For variety reasons, I also run shuttle-relay sprints. Place 4 baseballs 15 yards apart and shuttle-sprint back and forth. I will run a little distance, but not very much. I will continue to run sprints during the season and exercise on the LifeCycle bike. I do not do any heavy leg weight training. No squatting."

WEIGHT TRAINING

"During Spring Training, I will lift weights. Not heavy. Some upper body lifting, curls and light dumbbells for my arms. During the season, I will try and maintain my strength by lifting twice a week. No bench pressing. Lots of reps. My lifting exercises are: overhead triceps extensions, arm curls, leg curls, and leg extensions."

WARM-UP

"I believe in the loosen-up to warm-up to compete idea. I stretch in the club house before I take the field. Once I get out on the field, I run a few sprints to continue to loosen-up. I will then warm-up throwing, playing short toss/long toss catch. Once I feel that I am properly warmed up, I then head for the mound."

AT THE MOUND

"I continue to warm-up in the bullpen by first throwing in front of the mound. After I am pretty loose, I will then throw from behind the mound to stretch my arm. After my arm feels good, warm, and loose, I begin throwing from the rubber. I will throw approximately 60 pitches---mixing up my fast ball, curveball and change-up."

5-DAY ROTATION

"We have a 5-day rotation in Kansas City. My schedule for the week goes like this:

Day 1 "The first day is my scheduled start. My game routine is:
(1) stretch; (2) some sprints; (3) throwing the football; (4) short and long toss; (5) bullpen---warm-up throws in front of the mound and some throws behind the mound, then 60 pitches off the mound (60 pitches is abnormal, 50 pitches are enough for most big league pitchers).

Day 2 "The first day after I pitch, I do the following:
(1) weights; (2) stretch; (3) jog and sprints; (4) light catch, short toss.

Day 3 "The second day after I pitch, I do the following:
(1) stretch; (2) jog and sprints; (3) short toss and long toss.

Day 4 "The third day after I pitch, I do the following:
(1) weights; (2) stretch, jog and sprints; (3) short/long toss.

Day 5   "The fourth day after I pitch, I do the following:
(1) stretch; (2) jog and sprints; (3) short/long toss; (4) shag batting
practice; (5) play around---have fun.

Day 6   "This is my next scheduled day to pitch. (1) Same starter game
routine; (2) superstitious; (3) game face and attitude change,
positive thoughts; (4) review video of self against game day team;
and (5) go over game plan with pitching coach and catcher."

BULLPEN

"I am like Orel Hershiser. I do not throw a bullpen between starts. I feel
that I save wear and tear to my arm, less sore and tired, if I do not throw
a bullpen. If I am having a problem with a particular pitch, I will work
on it in the bullpen between starts."

ICING

"My personal preference is to ice my arm after every game and bullpen.
I ice my elbow and my shoulder for 20 minutes."

NO WIND-UP

"I do not have a wind-up. I want to get into the buried hands position and
be balanced at the top of my delivery before I go home. Therefore, I use
a no wind-up delivery. Balance and direction are the keys. The arm
swing overhead creates more moving parts to throw off my control. So
I have eliminated the arm swing."

THE STEP BACK

"I step straight back behind the rubber as I begin my no wind-up. I step
straight back because I want to stay in a direct line with home plate.
Also, I want to be in a balanced position after I post down into the hole,
before I stride forward to the plate. Balance and direction help my
control."

STRIDE

"My stride is a little unusual. I stride about 3-4 inches longer on my fastball than I do for my curveball."

IN THE STRETCH

"In the stretch, I want a compact set position. This will help me hold runners on, deliver quickly to the plate, if need be, and help my mechanics. The less wasted motion, the better are my mechanics and control."

THE TARGET

"I like to throw to a low target. I want my catcher to set the target early. I aim for the shin guards---in and out. I aim for the chest protector for up and in and away. I always aim for a part of the catcher's equipment."

HOLDING RUNNERS ON

"I always vary my looks. Sometimes I hold the ball longer, sometimes I rush to the plate faster, and sometimes I get a signal from our catchers when to throw over. Every pitcher must vary his move. I also use a quick slide step with a fast runner on first base. If I use this faster slide step, I usually throw my fastball. I always keep my hand and glove buried into my chest, so I can get rid of the ball quicker when throwing to first base."

CURVEBALL

"I do not set my curveball early like Blyleven. I choke it back in my hand and move a finger onto the seam. My fingers and wrist are sideways like shaking hands when releasing the ball (football spiral)."

CHANGE-UP

"I split my fingers, but I do not force the ball between them like a split-finger fastball. The split is not very wide. I also turn it over. I will not throw the split-finger."

SLIDER

"I will not throw the slider. I believe it will hurt my arm."

CUT FASTBALL

"I throw the cut fastball. I turn and cut my wrist a little, about one-half a notch at release. I take the same fastball grip."

SUPERSTITIOUS

"On the day I am going to pitch, I am very superstitious. I prepare for a good mental outlook. I also study my opposing hitters and my mechanics on video."

STRENGTH VS. STRENGTH

"Whenever I am in a strength vs. strength situation with a good hitter, I go with my best pitch. In these tight situations, I know I am going against the hitter's strength, such as a fastball hitter in a fastball situation. So I try and locate the fastball into his weak zone. When I need the strikeout or ground ball in tight situations, I LOCATE. I never want to lose a game with my second or third best pitch."

CONTROL DRILL

"I am a control pitcher. I believe I have always had good control because while growing up in California, I always was working on my control. As kids we used to throw between hung tires in trees, and make up control type games."

BOX SCORE

A pitcher doesn't throw, he pitches. He locates and changes speeds. We can't give everyone a Nolan Ryan arm. But we can improve everyone's mechanics for location and changing speeds. All winning pitchers locate and change speeds.

VII
Hitting Mechanics

*"Hitting is a fluid sequential motion
involving two movements working in tandem
---linear and then angular."*

--Dr. Coop DeRenne

"Hitting is the single most difficult thing to do in life," says Tommy Lasorda, L.A. Dodger manager. He rationalized that in life if a doctor, or attorney, or a teacher, etc., were successful only 30% of the time like a major league hitter (.300), then these professionals would be failures and likely out of business.

Hitting a baseball with all the "funny" spins and movements pitchers do is the single most difficult motor skill in all of sport. This is why on any baseball field and in any ball park hitting is discussed, theorized, and argued over more than any other baseball subject.

Picture or visualize if you can why hitting is so difficult. We are asking a normal untrained visual athlete while standing in the batter's box to hit an incoming round ball that could be fast, or slow, or breaking across, down or in, using a round bat as he tries to hit it squarely. Also, the hitter has the difficult task of trying to line up the two sweet spots on the ball (3/4") and bat (approx. 5") at the precise millisecond for a solid contact. To further complicate the problem are the facts that the hitter never sees the bat once it ballistically approaches the ball and the hitter visually loses sight of the ball anywhere from 6-15 feet out in front of the plate. In other words, the hitter cannot accurately guide the bat with his eyes and at the same time the ball is traveling too fast for his eyes to track it to the plate. He never sees the ball and bat make contact. Is it any wonder that hitting is so difficult?

Hitting: Science

You must always understand, in any movement, there is a PREPARATION, an EXECUTION, and a COMPLETION---a SEQUENCE. This sequence is a fluid flow of muscle contractions called COORDINATION. **The swing is composed of two sequential movements: (1) a weight shift forward, into (2) rotation. This fact is irrefutable.** After five years of research analyzing the best hitters in the big leagues using our high-tech Olympic Computerized Biomechanical Motion Analysis System at Bio-Kinetics, Inc., the results proved unequivocally that the swing is composed of two sequential movements---weight shift and then rotation.

⑪ *COACHING TIP*

Coach, when you break down the total swing into individual parts, you must never forget that NO ONE PART IS MORE IMPORTANT THAN THE WHOLE. That is why when you use different hitting drills in practice, you must be careful to use each drill in the context with the whole swing. You cannot isolate drills and individual parts of the swing. If you do, then the swing becomes robotic.

Coach, when you teach hitting, first, you must visualize the whole swing sequentially; and second, you must create in the minds of your players that the swing is a FLUID AND SEQUENTIAL MOVEMENT. No one part of the swing is more important than the other!

The Fluid Sequential Swing

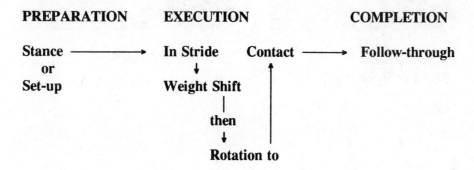

The above flow chart describes the two movements the body, the hands and bat go through during the entire swing. These two sequence and work together in tandem.

Don Mattingly:

The Stance
(Dynamic Balance)

The Stride

The Launch

The Approach

Bat Lag
(Knob to Ball)

Contact

Follow-Through

THE SWING

The Stance

Boston's Mike Greenwell

The starting stance should include the following:

- "A balance workable stance," says Charley Lau (ex-Kansas City Royals hitting instructor).

- The feet should be balanced with the weight (center of gravity, or CG) equally distributed between the feet. The feet should be about shoulder width apart and evenly aligned pointing at the pitcher. There should not be a leaning back on the back leg.

- The feet, knees, hips, shoulders, and head should be parallel and directionally pointing at the pitcher. The knees will be inside the feet, cocked a little.

- The head position is critical. The head should be facing the pitcher so that the hitter is looking at the pitcher with both eyes. It is now believed that even though we all have one dominant eye, both eyes are involved in the tracking process. There have not been any known cases in the big leagues where a hitter has hit successfully with only one eye. The point is, we live in a binocular world, so you must position your head throughout the swing in such a way as to take advantage of both eyes tracking the ball.

Therefore, the head and eyes from stance to contact should be in a stable position (no tilt) that would minimize head movement for more accuracy at contact. The important thing to remember is that the head and eyes must shift with no tilting from the release of the ball to the location where the hitter thinks the bat will intercept the ball.

It is a good idea to have your hitters develop the habit of tracking all pitches into the catcher's glove.

- The position of the bat must be held in such a way that the result is a compact swing. The bat should be held even or inside the shoulder, between 3-5 inches away from the body. The bat should be straight up or slightly tilted toward the back shoulder with the hands letter to shoulder high. The bat should be held comfortably in the fingers not in the palms.

- Do not change the hitter's stance or grip on the bat if he is comfortable unless the stance or grip hinders his swing.

The Stride

Boston's Mike Greenwell

The key points of the stride are as follows:

- **The stride should be a foot or less.** If the stride is longer than 12-15", then you are increasing the chance for a greater weight shift, which will cause the body and hands to lunge.

- Every time, the hitter should stride with a closed front toe. On every pitch, the stride is toward the pitcher with the same stride length.

- During the stride, the decision to swing or not is made. If the decision is to swing, then the front hip will begin to rotate the leg after the front heel plants down. **If the decision is to take the pitch, most great hitters take the pitch on the balls of their front landing foot-toes down and closed with the heel slightly raised (see the photo of Jose Conseco on page 152).** This position can be achieved by thinking that the stride is like stepping out onto thin ice or eggs.

⚾ *COACHING TIP*

To teach young hitters to be aggressive, have them ready to hit every pitch ("go vs. no go" philosophy). As they track the pitch, if it isn't their pitch, then they take it. The point is, they are swinging at every pitch until they decide that it is undesirable. This concept will teach them to be ready, concentrating on every pitch and be aggressive!

- The power in the swing comes from the Kinetic Link Principle. As the hips rotate, energy is transferred through the body sequentially from one body part to the next, resulting in a high bat velocity. **Therefore, power is generated from hip rotation, not strong arms and fast hands.**

- The head and eyes should remain level during the stride. It is impossible for the head to remain still.

- As the hitter strides forward, the hands and bat will move slightly back---**"walking away from your hands."** In other words, the hands go back as the lower half of the body strides forward. The bat will remain in the vicinity of the rear shoulder, not behind it, if at all possible. The farther the hands and bat move back, the farther the bat has to travel forward in the approach.

The Launch Position

Wade Boggs   *Don Mattingly*

At the end of the stride, the body is in the launch position ready to swing the bat, or take the pitch. The characteristics of a good launch are as follows:

- If the hitter has decided to swing the bat, during the stride the front hip begins to rotate the leg as the lead foot-heel plants down. This planting action signals the hip extensor muscles to extend the knee into a firm blocking position.

- If the hitter decides to take the pitch, during the stride the hitter will land on the ball of his front foot (toes down, and heel slightly raised) while holding his hands back in the launch position. Again, this foot action is like stepping out onto thin ice.

- As the "hands walk away" from the body during the stride and the hitter leaves the hands near the back shoulder, the back elbow usually automatically raises up. The important point is that the hands should remain close to the back shoulder. Let the elbow move upward naturally. Do not wrap the bat barrel over the head with the bat pointing at the pitcher.

- The position of the hands and bat in the launch position are very important. **They should be near the back shoulder, not behind it, with the bat angling toward the rear shoulder or head. The hands will remain close to the shoulder and chest, no more than three to five inches away from the body. Again, do not wrap the bat barrel.**

Jose Conseco
(Taking a Pitch)

The Approach

George Bell
(Bat Lag)

Roberto Clemente
(Knob to the Ball)

The approach is the route that the bat takes from the launch position to contact. The bat and hands route in the approach should go this way:

- As the proper launch position has been obtained, the last link of the kinetic link kicks in---the BAT LAG.

- The upper body sequentially rotates in the following manner: hips, shoulders, and trunk. After the upper body rotates, the bat is brought forward in a linear (straight) route. The verbal cue coaches should use is **"Take the knob to the ball."** First, the bat approaches the contact zone in a horizontal bat lag position; then it goes angular or rotates when the wrists are uncocked.

  This horizontal lag position produces high bat velocity because the bat has not been casted outward creating a longer traveling distance to contact. Also, because the bat is traveling first in a straight path, the hitter will be more accurate at contact.

⚾ *COACHING TIP*

Teach your young hitters that the route of the bat in the approach is ALWAYS the same on every pitch no matter where the ball is located. Therefore, in practices, young hitters must practice taking the knob of the bat to every pitch location.

PATH OF HANDS AND BAT: To achieve this bat route, the swing is basically **LEVEL to DOWNWARD.** The bat will level out only on a pitch below the letters and above the waist. The barrel will be even or higher than the hands as the bat approaches contact. This downward bat route will create back spin on the ball at contact much like a golf ball in flight. This adds carry and distance to the flight of the baseball.

Contact

Tony Gwynn   *Babe Ruth*

The following things occur at contact:

- Mechanically, the body is a balanced position and fully rotated.

- Visually, the hitter must be in the best mechanical or physical position to track the baseball. If the hitter is balanced and has rotated properly, the head will be in the best tracking position.

- **Visually, the body must help position the head and eyes into the most advantageous tracking position. The head should never tilt during the swing. As the ball is released, the head and eyes move naturally or downward following the flight of the ball.**

- **The hitter's CG (center of gravity; weight-at belly button) is equally distributed between both feet.** The front leg is firm and extended with the toes pointing at a 45 degree angle toward the pitcher. The backside leg has formed a reverse "L" at the knee joint with the upper and lower leg; and a reverse "L" at the ankle joint. The backside shoe laces and toes are pointing downward. If these leg positions have been achieved, the body will be balanced and fully rotated.

- The arms are slightly bent at impact. They do not reach extension. But, coach, the goal to try to hit the ball out in front of the plate is important, therefore have your hitters try to get extension at impact.

- The hands at contact are underneath the bat. The palm of the leading bottom hand is facing downward and the palm of the top hand is facing upward. The wrists are not broken or rolling over.

The Follow-Through

Rod Carew

Babe Ruth

- Impact has occurred and the ball has left the bat. The body must be in a balanced position, fully rotated.

- The arms and bat will finish naturally and approximately shoulder height.

- Some coaches advocate releasing the top hand just after contact. This is a controversial subject. Remember, the ball has left the bat. Releasing the top hand after contact does not effect the flight of the ball in any way. It is up to the hitter if he wants to release his top hand first, or release both hands at the finish of the follow-through. This is a matter of personal preference.

MENTAL HITTING

A good mental hitter has the following characteristics: (1) confidence, (2) visual awareness (concentration), and (3) aggressiveness.

Confidence

Every good hitter has no fear. He believes he can hit anyone. He believes in his mechanics and knows he is well prepared. He is confident with every at bat.

His confidence comes from the coach and within himself. Coach, prepare your hitters properly and constantly give them positive affirmations in practices and in games. This will help build confidence in your hitters. Without confidence a hitter is an automatic out---INFORM, INSTRUCT and INSPIRE.

Confidence is a learned and acquired feeling. If a hitter focuses his attention on his visual skills during the game, he will improve his ball-bat contact skill (eye-hand coordination). If he is making more solid contacts, his confidence increases.

Visual Awareness

Mental hitting is really the concentration of one's visual skills during his time at bat. Every hitter must understand that while at the plate the only thing that counts is his visual awareness skills. Mechanics are secondary. If the hitter is not tuned into his **visual system** at the plate, then his contact accuracy is retarded. Good mechanics are not enough to get the job done.

⚾ *COACHING TIP*

> *Again, DeRenne's Laws of Competitive Performance:*
>
> *1. NEVER TEACH MECHANICAL SKILLS IN A GAME.*
> *2. PUT THE PLAYER IN THE VISUAL SYSTEM.*

In practice, the hitter should: (1) demonstrate his stop-freeze body position at swing contact; and (2) demonstrate his slow motion entire swing. If he demonstrates poor mechanics, then, coach, you must first teach him visualization (a picture in his mind of the correct swing). How?: (1) the hitter watches daily a slow motion video of good hitting mechanics (Rod Carew's Sybervision videotape); and (2) you must video the hitter's mechanics and compare his swing to the models.

The visual process at the plate is as follows: (1) visualize your good swing before you step into the batter's box; (2) in the box, center on the ball at release---read the spin of the ball; (3) track the ball to the plate and into the catcher's glove; (4) after every pitch, ask yourself if the ball was slow and big as a beach ball; (5) clear your mind after every pitch, only concentrating on your visual system; and (6) after every at bat, ask yourself: "Did I pick-up the ball from the pitcher's hand; did I swing or hit a strike or good pitch; did I take a pitch I should have swung at; did I have two or three good swings; did I track the ball clearly to the plate; was I aggressive and confident?"

Coach, if you are stressing to your hitters in the games visual dynamics, visualization, centering on the ball at release, and the tracking process, then the minds of the hitters in the batter's box will be concentrating only on their visual skills. Therefore, they will not be thinking or worried. Fear and thinking retard the visual system at the plate.

Aggressiveness

Coach, teach the hitter to be aggressive. Again, the concept of "go vs. no go." Every hitter is ready to swing at every pitch. If the pitch is undesirable, then they take the pitch while tracking it into the catcher's glove. The hitter's bat speed will be maximized if he is ready to swing at every pitch. He will not have a lazy bat. In batting practice, preach aggressiveness. Swing at only good pitches, strikes.

There should be more 3-0 count swings at the youth baseball level. This will help you teach aggressiveness and at the same time, instill confidence in your hitters.

BOX SCORE

To become a good hitter, you first must be a smart hitter. Learn the strike zone as well as the mechanics of the swing. Remember, swing mechanics and visual skills go hand-in-glove together.

VIII
Team Play

"The team is made up of individuals,
functioning together in unity."

--Dr. Coop DeRenne

TEAM OFFENSE

In one word, team offense means **AGGRESSIVE** attack. Team offense is based on three factors:

- power
- speed
- balance: power and speed with pitching

159

If you have team power, then you play for the big inning. Be patient and wait for the explosion. If you have speed merchants, then you play "Billy Ball" (Billy Martin style of play). **You manufacture runs.** Usually, this kind of offense is used when you have team speed and a good pitching staff. Create pressure on the defense. Make things happen. Always look for the extra base. Challenge the defense's arms.

If you have a combination of power and speed in your offense, a well-balanced attack up and down the line-up, then sit back and watch the game. Be patient with this offense and give the players the green light with some expert guidance from you. You should win more than you lose.

DeRenne's Offensive Rules:

- **The concept of TEAM is a result of players executing individually.** If all the players know their strengths and roles, then team runs and team wins will take care of themselves. **Execution scores runs and wins games, not having all hearts and minds think team first.**

- Do not ask a player to do something that he is not capable of executing and/or that which you have not prepared him to do. You will be creating a high failure to success ratio. You will be instilling negative thinking in your player. Normally, if he fails, then we blame the player. This is wrong. Realistically, coach, it was your fault that he failed.

  > EXAMPLE: If you have not been bunting in practice, then do not expect the perfect bunt in an adrenalin-rush pressured situation. If your third hitter is coming up in a bunt situation, and he has not bunted all season, don't ask him to bunt. Ask him to do what he does best.

- **Again, baseball is a team sport made up of individuals. Prepare each player for a certain role in your offense.** This role is based on the player's strengths. Once you have identified your players' strengths, then develop your offensive philosophy and team plays. Next, create your lineup. PUT THE HORSE BEFORE THE CART.

- The lineup from top to bottom will reflect your players' strengths, offensive philosophy and team play.

- Find your basic lineup core or nucleus early in the season. This group will provide the majority of your offense. **Count on this group under pressure.**

- **Nurture your substitutes.** Work your "subs" into your offense slowly. Give them room to succeed first before you count on them in the "clutch." It is vital for team harmony that the subs know their respective roles.

- The Offensive Chart: Devise an offensive chart which will show the true worth of the players' game performance. **Remember, the two most important offensive statistics are ON-BASE PERCENTAGE AND ADVANCING RUNNERS.**

The hitter's objectives as he approaches the plate are as follows: (1) First, if there are base runners ahead of him, then he should try and advance the runners to score; and (2) he must then try to get on base. Then, the next goal of this hitter/base runner is to score a run. Therefore, on-base percentages and advancing runners are critical statistics that a coach must look at when developing his team offensive attack.

⑪ *COACHING TIP*

Runs are a function of runners' advancement percentage plus on-base percentage.

TEAM DEFENSE

Someone said, "The best defense is a good offense." But, what if your team can't hit...

Defense is the key to a sound and solid team. It is the number one ingredient to winning. Good defense helps the pitching staff more than a good offense. First, build your team defensively, then offensively. How?...

<u>Leadership</u>: Build leadership qualities within your catcher, shortstop and center fielder. Teach them to think for themselves and learn how to adjust to each new game situation. Thinking and adjusting are two important trainable skills that all successful athletes share.

<u>Defensive skills</u>: Throwing and catching are much easier to develop within your players than hitting. If you just concentrate on the basic fundamentals of catching, throwing, and fielding ground balls and fly balls, your defense will be noticeably improved. It is when you try and add new complicated defensive plays that the total defense breaks down.

In every practice, all players must work on their defense. **Again, the most important defensive aspect to work on is the basic defensive fundamentals. Just as important as teaching fundamentals, you must teach "game defensive sense."** All defensive players must be taught to know each other's responsibilities in any given situation. Also, they all must be taught where and how to move during the defensive plays. This game sense is developed in practice under simulated game conditions. At least a couple of times a week, teach game sense defensive responsibilities.

<u>Remember, do not expect your players to play like adults</u>. Do not give them defensive plays that are above their mental and physical abilities. Keep the defenses simple, but work hard in executing the basics of each rudimentary defense.

<u>"Be strong down the middle</u>." You all have heard this old adage before. This defensive philosophy is true. Your strengths defensively lie down the middle of the field: catcher, shortstop, second baseman, and center fielder. Daily, develop their defensive mechanics and their game awareness or instincts. All defensive plays will revolve around these key players.

<u>Heads up</u>: All defensive players must be ready on every pitch. They must be taught the proper ready fielding positions and how to move and read the oncoming batted ball. They must be taught how to **adjust** to every new game situation. Therefore, the defense should look for cues or clues from the coach or from the surrounding situation in order to know what defense to execute. The defense should recognize what to do based on the following:

- outs and inning
- score
- base runners
- hitter's speed and hitting tendencies
- pitcher's control
- opposing team's type of offense
- own defensive strengths and weaknesses

Defensive Charts: Coaches should chart the opposing team hitters' speeds and hitting tendencies. Note the opposing team's type of offense; who bunts, who hits and runs, who steals, etc. Set the team defense according to the opposing team's offense. **PLAN YOUR WORK AND WORK YOUR PLAN!**

As your defense improves, so will your pitching. Good defense makes the pitchers better. Every day, work on the normal routine plays. The lack of executing the routine play causes more losses than not making the great game play.

HUSTLE: **Do not require hustle, DEMAND HUSTLE. IT TAKES NO TALENT TO HUSTLE.**

⑪ *COACHING TIP*

MORE YOUTH BASEBALL GAMES ARE LOST THAN WON! Work on the basic fundamentals with your team and you will have a chance to be "in" every game.

BOX SCORE

Keep the offense and defense simple. The result will be higher execution.

A team begins with individuals executing individually. Therefore, a TEAM is a collection of players and executions working in unity. The goal of the team plan is teaching players to execute under pressure. Keep the team plans simple.

IX
Troubleshooting

"Problem identification is half the solution."

There are many ways to look at troubleshooting. The simplest method is based on the following philosophical idea: Problem identification is half the solution. You must identify the problem correctly, not guess. Use high-tech equipment or expert authorities' information. Do not guess or assume. In other words, "TREAT THE ILLNESS, NOT THE SYMPTOM."

Parents and coaches, you all live with the frustrations of these young players everyday. It seems that everyday is a new day, and a new problem. **Just remember, it is not the quantity of problems, IT IS THE QUALITY OF THE SOLUTION that you arrive at that will make you a better coach or parent.** Do not dwell on or worry about the number of problems that you face. Go right to the illness---cure the illness and the symptoms will disappear.

PITCHING

The Curveball

When you tell the young pitcher, do not throw curves, the minute you turn your back he will be throwing breaking pitches. Over the last ten years, the baseball communities were led to believe that the curveball caused injuries in young players' arms. Over the last five years, exercise science and biomechanical research supports the fact that if the young pitcher develops the proper pitching and grip mechanics, if his arm has been properly conditioned, and if his coaches prevent an overuse of game curveballs, then with good information and proper monitoring by his coach, he can throw curveballs at approximately 15 years of age.

We realize league rules allow a player to throw a curveball at a young age. Regardless, coaches develop the fastball and change-up early on with your pitchers. Always remember, a good change-up "sets up" the fastball and curveball. If a pitcher starts throwing the curveball at a very early age, he may never really develop his fastball and change-up. He will become over dependent with his curveball.

Mechanics: Remember, the body mechanics of throwing the curveball are the same as with the fastball. The only difference is the position of the forearm and wrist, and finger placement on the ball at release.

When first learning the curveball, have the young pitcher put three fingers inside the upside down horseshoe of the baseball seam. Reinforce in him the karate-chop motion of the wrist and forearm at release.

When you get into the launch position, and accelerate the arm forward, karate-chop the baseball at release. Do not twist the arm, or spin the fingers. **The karate-chop grip puts the fingers into a supinated position like a hammer chop with a firm wrist and forearm.** Therefore, when the arm automatically snaps straight at release, there will be little or no stress on the elbow. If you do not try and twist or spin your fingers, there will be little or no stress on the elbow. What causes elbow bone, ligament, and tendon problems is the twisting or spinning of the fingers and wrist rotation as the arm reaches full extension at release.

The Curveball

Icing Controversy

It is not a controversy. It is a choice. Medical studies reveal that healthy arms, while throwing a baseball, will produce micro-tears and bleeding in the muscle tissues and capillaries. Icing will "slow down" the micro-tears and the bleeding.

There are two kinds of stiffness: (1) There is stiffness and soreness from micro-tears and the actual pounding on a muscle; and (2) There is stiffness from the chemical lactic acid buildup in the muscle tissues that occurs with fatigue and muscle failure. The two kinds of stiffness cause a double-edge sword effect. Repetitious throwing in a game is causing micro-tears and bleeding in the muscle tissues; and the lactic acid buildup causes the muscles to fatigue and become stiff and possibly sore.

Medically, ice will retard the bleeding. It will also slow down that stiffness and soreness that is a result of the bleeding of the capillaries and muscle tissues.

Concurrently, we recommend while icing the arm, have your pitchers do some form of aerobic work. A stationary bike is best, because it will also help "change the oil" aerobically after a game or bullpen session. We have found that the stationary bike works best for the elite major league pitcher. This does the following two things: (1) the ice impeded the bleeding of the micro-tears and muscle tissue; and (2) the aerobic work changes the oil by flushing out the lactic acid chemical buildup that is associated with muscle stiffness and fatigue. At the major league level, it reduces "bounce-back" time or the recovery period for the pitcher considerably. Therefore, the stiffness and soreness that the pitcher normally feels have been diminished considerably by icing and biking concurrently in post-workout and post-game exercise sessions.

If there is not a stationary bike available, the young athlete could lie on his back with his legs up in the air in a bicycle position and pump his legs for 15 minutes during this icing period. Treading water in a pool while holding onto a kickboard is another example of aerobic work a young player can do while icing.

⊕ *COACHING TIP*

Coach and parents, ICE BOTH THE SHOULDER AND THE ELBOW FOR ONLY 15 MINUTES IMMEDIATELY AFTER THE GAME OR PRACTICE BULLPEN.

Sore Arms

The sports medicine community reveals that there are three physical conditions that contribute to a sore arm: (1) poor pitching mechanics; (2) overuse workloads: number of pitches in a week; and (3) an improper conditioning base that should support the pitcher's workloads and his mechanical efficiency. If any one of the three above conditions are functionally less than optimal, then a breakdown will occur, resulting in a stiff or sore arm.

Stiffness is defined as a slight uncomfortable feeling that will go away when the young pitcher loosens up to warm up to do his activity.

Soreness is defined as an injury. And no matter how much you loosen up or warm up to do your activity, the soreness does not go away.

A young pitcher should **NEVER BE ASKED TO COMPETE WHEN HE IS SORE.** But, at the same time, the young pitcher must understand the difference between a stiff or sore arm. You must teach your young pitchers this difference. Your pitchers must understand that there will be a certain amount of stiffness associated with pitching, but their stiffness must go away if they warm up and loosen up properly. If the stiffness does not go away after they warm up and loosen up, then they have a sore arm, and you treat it like an injury-rest and no throwing. If they understand these principles, then they will not have a fear of injury.

The arm has its own line of defense against injuries. The first line of defense against a sore arm are muscles. The second line of defense are the tendons and ligaments attaching the muscles to muscles or muscles to bones. And the third line of defense in the arm are the bones.

If a young pitcher is not conditioned properly and not strong enough to handle his mechanics in the number of throws asked out of his arm weekly, then he will possibly experience tendonitis, inflammation of ligaments, and possibly bursitis that goes along with joint problems. Therefore, if you have joint and connective tissue problems, it just means you are not strong enough.

When muscles, tendons and ligaments are not strong enough to handle the pitcher's workloads and his mechanical inefficiency, then you break bone. When the bone is broken or deteriorates, calcium deposits and stress fractures appear. Our friend, Dave Dravecky, ex-pitcher of the San Francisco Giants, is an example of a well-conditioned pitcher that did not have enough muscle tissue to decelerate his arm after an extensive rehabilitation program. The cancer in his arm ate away his muscle tissue, and no matter how much rehabilitation and strength building he did to his muscles, tendons and ligaments, he still broke his arm under competitive conditions that ended his career.

Most shoulder problems or injuries occur in the deceleration of the arm after the releasing of the ball. The backside or posterior shoulder has one less throwing muscle group than the anterior or front side. The posterior shoulder decelerates the arm in half the time it takes the arm to accelerate when throwing a baseball. In other words, there are three muscle groups that accelerate the throwing arm in X amount of time and there are only two muscle groups that decelerate the arm in half X amount of time.

With every throw, the posterior shoulder is always "paying" for this muscle imbalance. Therefore, in the conditioning process to keep the shoulder from getting injured, whatever exercise workload volume is used for the anterior shoulder, the posterior shoulder muscles need one-third more volume.

> EXAMPLE: If a pitcher exercises the anterior shoulder muscles by doing 10 pushups, then he needs to do 13 body dips for the posterior shoulder muscles.

Surgeries

Anytime a surgery is recommended by two orthopedists, a player should work out before or pre-condition the body for the surgery. In other words, the injured player should strength train to tolerance before surgery, as long as it doesn't exacerbate the problem. If the player is stronger going into surgery, this will help reduce his rehabilitation or "bounce back" time after the surgery. Consult with your orthopedic about strength prior to surgery.

After the surgery, the player begins to rehabilitate the arm by strength training. As the player strength trains during his rehabilitation, first the muscles become stronger than the tendons and ligaments. Also, during rehabilitation, the tendons and ligaments do not receive as much blood, oxygen and nutrients as the muscle tissue. Therefore, while the player acquires the lost strength that he had prior to surgery during normal rehabilitation, he should continue to strength train an extra two to three weeks to gain connective tissue strength.

This extra strength training period during rehabilitation will provide the proper balance of strength in the weak connective tissue areas with the stronger corresponding muscles in the arm. In other words, because the muscles will gain strength sooner than tendon and ligament strength, the player needs extra rehabilitation time to strengthen the corresponding weaker connective tissues before he can ever compete again.

The throwing rehabilitation process should begin only after the player has been tested for the right amount of muscle and connective tissue strength. This will help reduce the risk factor in the overall rehabilitation.

⚾ *COACHING TIP:*

> *Coach, you must understand, a pitcher coming off surgery should never build muscle strength and muscle endurance while throwing from a mound during rehabilitation. The act of throwing down a slope off the mound is a tearing down process. During the throwing rehabilitation process, all throwing should be done on flat ground in athletic tennis shoes.*
>
> *Gradually, during the throwing rehabilitation, the pitcher will work his way to the mound with spikes. Once he finally reaches the mound, you should have the catcher move in front of the plate as the pitcher begins to get used to throwing down the slope of the mound. Once the pitcher shows added strength and endurance and familiarity throwing off the mound at this shortened distance, then he can begin throwing over the regulation distance.*

Pitch Totals

The fatigue barometer for a pitcher should be **THE NUMBER OF PITCHES, NOT THE NUMBER OF INNINGS.** As a rule of thumb, based upon 20 years of pitching and coaching in professional baseball and working with youth league pitchers in the off-season over the last two decades, **a young pitcher should not throw more than 75 pitches in a game.**

We also recommend that, if at all possible, once a young pitcher pitches 3 innings or 30 plus pitches, he should not throw again until he has rested for a minimum of 4-5 days. If a pitcher throws his maximum of 75 pitches, he should rest a full week before he pitches again.

Before a game, the warm-up routine for a pitcher must follow this safety sequence: (1) stretch for 10 minutes; (2) light jogging for a few minutes; (3) play short/long toss catch on flat ground for 5 to 7 minutes until the arm feels comfortably loose and warm; and (4) continue to warm up, throwing off the mound for 35 to 40 pitches.

The pitcher times this warm-up process just before he goes into the game. Usually, he rests about 3 to 5 minutes before he enters the game and takes his inning warm-up throws.

⚾ *COACHING TIP:*

> *Coach, not only monitor the number of pitches your pitcher throws over the course of the game, but also the intensity of the pitches. Determine when fatigue sets in; and especially watch carefully for the intensive inning where the total of pitches is excessively high. These are "red flag" warnings to remove your pitcher from the game, so as to reduce the possibility of injury.*

Bullpen

At the big league level with a five-man pitching rotation, the starting pitcher will throw his mid-week bullpen THREE DAYS AFTER the day he pitched. **Physiologically, it takes approximately 72 hours for the body to flush out all the micro-tear bleedings, old and dead nutrients, and lactic acid buildup while recovering from muscle fatigue, stiffness and soreness.**

Again, the two days following a pitching outing are used for weight training and aerobic work called "changing the oil" for the upcoming bull-pen and next start. During these two days, there will be light throwing from flat ground. Coach, you should understand that the purpose of this rest period is to give the pitcher needed rest from throwing off the mound.

Bullpens, or skill work, should only be done when there is no stiffness or soreness in the pitcher's arm. All bullpens should be CLEAN, CRISP AND QUICK. Bullpens are used for tune-ups. Starting pitchers should only throw one bullpen between starts. During a normal bullpen, the starting pitcher should throw approximately **50 pitches.**

We might add, because throwing off a mound is a tearing down process, some successful big league starting pitchers do not throw a bullpen between starts. Cy Young winners Bret Saberhagen and Orel Hershiser believe they will save wear and tear on their arms if they eliminate the mid-week bullpens between starts. They will throw in the bullpen, if they feel they need control work, if they need extra work on a troubled pitch, or while they are learning a new pitch.

At the big league level, relief pitchers' bullpens and skill work are handled differently than the starting pitchers. In three out of four days, or in four out of six days, relievers will throw from the mound, but they will only throw 25 pitches at a pop as a light tune-up.

Trips to the Mound

Coach, when you are going to the mound in the middle of the inning during the game, it means he is struggling. You must identify why he is scuffling.

Walk out and settle him down by first giving him some positive affirmations. Hopefully, this will help him to clear his mind and remove some of the pressure. Next, give him concrete visual reinforcement information.

With a clear mind as he toes the rubber, he is to concentrate only on the target. This will be his signal to center only on the target. **Hitting the target is the only thing that is important.** You must permit the pitcher to allow his body to do what it has prepared to do. **You can't change his skill mechanics at this moment, so let him pitch with the confidence you gave him as he concentrates only on hitting the target.**

The worst thing you can do is to be a teacher at this point or an angry coach. Coach, motivational or creative speeches won't work because they will distract his attention from his visual job. More often than not, he got into trouble because of mental reasons and not because of mechanical problems. Therefore, encourage him, calm him down, and most important, help him to concentrate only on hitting the target.

If he fails, you remove him from the game with some encouraging words. Then you focus on the next relief pitcher. After the game, or the next day in practice, you must talk to him privately. In practice, you give him specific skill work for him to correct his mechanical problem. Again, SEE IT, FEEL IT, DO IT.

<u>When to Relieve?</u>

Whitey Herzog, ex-manager of the St. Louis Cardinals, said it best: "The hardest thing a manager has to do is to realize when to go to the relief pitcher."

When to go to the relief pitcher is pure judgment. To help you make this most difficult decision, here are some concrete suggestions:

- Look at the total number of pitches thrown up to this point.

- Look for a particular inning for an excessive amount of pitches thrown.

- Signs of fatigue: (1) the pitcher is taking extra time between pitches; (2) there are numerous breaks in his rhythm; (3) he is dropping down and throwing side arm from his normal delivery; (4) he physically looks tired, into muscle failure; and (5) a noticeable drop in velocity.

- Look at his mental approach. Is he beat mentally?

THE DILEMMA: You do not want to jerk his sheets too quickly, and yet on the other hand, you do not want to leave him in too long and have his confidence get buried.

If you have worked hard to prepare your pitcher to compete, you will know your pitcher. You will have a feeling why he is struggling, whether he can get through this trouble, or it's time to go to the relief pitcher. In other words, you have to know your pitcher, recognize that it is a mental or physical problem, and then make the decision accordingly.

Game Day Preparation

Diet: Coach, youth baseball is not the big leagues. Let the young player eat what he wants on game day with only this one qualification. **Have him stay away from refined carbohydrates---sugars.** Sweets will raise the blood sugar level too high too fast, causing him first to be hyperactive, and then later on, after the blood sugar drops excessively, he will become sluggish and fatigued. Remember, it is very difficult to monitor a young player's diet.

Mental Preparation: **Have a short meeting with the team before the game and remind them that they have worked hard all week in practice and now it is time to have some fun.**

Try and take the players' nervousness and pressure away from them. Demand that your players hustle, be aggressive, and be alert at all times. Above all, they must enjoy the game.

Coach, youth baseball must first be **FUN. Skill and behavioral development is second, and a very, very distant third or fourth is winning and losing.**

Warm-Up: The warm-up sequence on game day for all players is the same as for practices: loosen up to warm up to do your activity. (1) Loosen up with a little stretching and a little jogging; (2) continue warming up on flat ground, then go into short/long toss baseball throwing.

⚾ *COACHING TIP*

All pitchers should cover their elbows with an undersleeve shirt. Research reveals that the best baseball sleeve is made by Clutch Co., Inc., Honolulu, Hawaii.

The Clutch Co.
Baseball Sleeve

Diagnosis and Prescription

In diagnosing the mechanical pitching delivery flaw, we must first treat the illness (the four pitching absolutes) and then the secondary symptoms will disappear. Therefore, there are four check points in the delivery sequence that must be looked at carefully to see if there has been a breakdown in the four absolutes.   These check points are as follows: (1) balance at the post position; (2) at stride foot-plant; (3) at ball release; and (4) the deceleration route of the throwing arm.

At these check points, first determine if the absolutes have been violated. If so, then correct the absolute by correcting the body segment and the problems should disappear.

The majority of mechanical pitching flaws lies in three main areas: (1) unbalance at the post position; (2) rushing through the delivery; and (3) a recoiling action in the follow-through.

If a pitcher is experiencing one of these last two problems, then he has increased his susceptibility to a major arm injury. Rushing through the delivery may cause a premature opening up of the front "directional" side leading to anterior shoulder, rotator cuff, and medial elbow problems during arm acceleration. A recoiling or incomplete follow-through after ball release may cause a posterior shoulder injury during arm deceleration.

Mechanical Problem 1: The "Wobbler"

Problem Recognition:

The slight wobbler is unbalanced at the top of his delivery. He is leaning on his back-posting leg (flexed back leg), or slightly leaning to one of the foul lines. He is in this unbalanced position (not noticeable to him) because he has kicked or swung up his front side directional leg (stride leg), so that the foot is either pointing at the opposite foul line or swung back past the rubber. In either case, he must now lean back sideways or back toward second base to counterbalance this unbalanced position.

Problem Sequence Identification:

- At post position: absolute flaw = balance

- During the pivot: anatomical flaw = kicking up or out, or a swinging away and back of front side leg.

- At post position: collapse of back pivot leg; leaning back (to foul line or second base) of body while fighting balance.

Solution:

• **Teach a quadricep ("quad") lift.** The pitcher lifts his quad as he pivots down. As he lifts his quad, he must tuck his lower leg (knee to foot) underneath the quad, so that he has a 90 degree bend at the knee and his foot is pointing down as he reaches the highest point in the leg lift.

• The wall drill: Have the pitcher stand parallel and close to a wall as he goes through his delivery. The wall should prevent him from kicking up or swinging up and extending out his front leg as pivots down.

• Hands-on: As he swings up his leg, stop this action and hold him by the foot. Place his lower leg underneath his knee with the foot pointing to the ground. Next, back him into the pivoting down action, and help him lift the quad up to the new balanced position at the top of his delivery. As he lifts his quad, teach him to time this action with a coming down movement of the hands into his comfort zone (chest area). This is the correct post-balanced position before initiating the stride forward.

The Wall Drill

Mechanical Problem 2: The "Rusher"

Problem Recognition:

The "rusher" exhibits a premature opening up of the front side (especially the hips and shoulder) as he strides forward to the plate. This premature rotation is evident while the stride leg is in the air.

Problem Sequence Identification:

- At stride leg foot-plant: absolute flaw = Direction; Weight Transfer.

- At post position: anatomical problem = hands and body never stop for one beat of balance.

- In stride and at front foot-plant: anatomical problem = early rotation of front side hip and shoulder.

Solution:

- **Teach the pitcher to bring hands to chest (comfort zone) and pause one second at the post position before striding toward the plate.** This will also help his balance and direction.

- Use surgical tubing. Tie a stretch cord shoulder height on a fence. The pitcher stretches the cord out from the fence as he strides out holding the cord in his throwing hand. As he strides away from the fence, he must concentrate on keeping his front side directional toward the plate, and not to prematurely open up the hips and shoulders until foot-plant.

- Hands-on: Put your hands on his hips (from the rear) as he strides forward not allowing him to prematurely open up his hips.

Mechanical Problem 3: The "Recoiler"

Problem Recognition:

The recoiler exhibits a recoiling action or an incomplete arm follow-through route after releasing the ball. After ball release, the hand and arm stop at the waist and fail to continue through the deceleration range of motion.

Solution:

- Teach the pitcher that he must complete his follow-through by taking his hand across his body and down past his landing leg knee. **"Pick-up dirt"** is your verbal cue.

- **Have the pitcher try and bury his nose in the catcher's glove after he releases the ball.** This directional action will force the pitcher to properly complete his follow-through route.

- Hands-on: Walk through the pitcher's delivery with him. Guide the path of his arm after ball release through its deceleration route.

⑪ *COACHING TIP*

We all learn by our senses: SEE IT, FEEL IT, DO IT. Slow motion and walking speeds in the hands-on bullpen sessions are vital to the accelerated learning process.

HITTING

Practice Philosophy: Diagnosis and Prescription

Again, the objective for practices is to develop the players' skills. The objectives for the game are to have fun and to gain experience, not to develop skills.

When analyzing a hitter, because it is the most difficult skill in the world to execute, your analysis must be correct. **Therefore, before you correctly diagnose, you must determine if the problem is mechanical or visual, or mental.** You must determine: (1) Is the hitter deciding to swing the bat at the right time (mental and visual; (2) Is he tracking the ball clearly all the way (visual); (3) Does the hitter know the strike zone (mental and visual); (4) Does he have confidence or is he afraid at the plate (mental); and (5) Is the batter's swing mechanics hindering his hitting performance (mechanical). **Once you determine the illness, then you can properly treat the hitter.**

If you have determined that a player is having swing mechanical problems, you should have arrived at this assumption from watching his game performances. Therefore, you must watch his mechanics over the course of a few games to see if he is consistently making the same mechanical mistake(s), assuming his problem is mechanical. To determine the real "illness" in his swing, use a video camera. Remember, THE HAND IS QUICKER THAN THE EYE, BUT THE CAMERA DOES NOT LIE."

In practice, give this struggling hitter **swing-specific drills** to correct his mechanical problem. Remember, specific skill repetitions are necessary when learning a new skill as well as when trying to break old habits. You must be patient with hitters and you must use positive affirmations.

If the hitter is afraid of the ball, the hitting problem is mental (i.e., stepping into the bucket or bailing out). You must use a softer imitation baseball to help him overcome his fear. Then, as his fear goes away, work on his mechanics. **Do not try and conquer his fear and mechanical flaw at the same time.**

A hitter can be making poor decisions at the plate that have nothing to do with poor mechanics. Two common examples of wrong decisions at the plate are as follows: (1) His bat arrives late at contact---he seems to always be fouling off or missing mediocre pitches in the game or in batting practice---he is not deciding in time to begin his swing; and (2) He is constantly swinging at bad pitches in the game as well as in batting practice---he does not know the strike zone.

Coach, you should give him centering and tracking drills during practice which will help him center on the ball at release and help him track the ball to the bat. When he improves his centering and tracking skills, he will be able to make better decisions: (1) Is the pitch a strike or a ball; and (2) When should I start my swing.

Game Philosophy: Diagnosis and Prescription

Again, let the players play the game. Do not instruct. Emphasize that they must stay visual at the plate. Do not let them turn on their physical channel.

At the plate, if your hitters are concentrating on your mechanical swing instructions, or a particular part of their body, then this physical channel will retard their centering and tracking skills. **YOUR PLAYERS MUST UNDERSTAND THAT THEIR SINGULAR OBJECTIVE WHILE AT THE PLATE IS TO CONCENTRATE ONLY ON THEIR CENTERING AND TRACKING SKILLS.**

Again, coach, you should emphasize the visual system during the game by asking visual questions to your hitters. Your players must forget their mechanics in the game. In practice, work on their hitting mechanics.

If you have players that are struggling at the plate, put them in a position in the batting order that they might have a better chance of success.

> EXAMPLE: Your best hitter is turning his head while tracking the ball, and he is "taking his eye off the ball." Take some pressure off of him and bat him farther down in the order. Do not take him out of the lineup. He must hit his way out of his slump. Continuously, keep giving him positive affirmations and show confidence in him.

Game Application: Diagnosis and Prescription

This section deals with identifying the mechanical flaw in the swing and prescribing the correct treatment. The most difficult job for the hitting coach and the hitter is to correctly identify the exact mechanical flaw (illness) that causes the poor performance. Most coaches treat the symptom---the secondary problem which usually is a body segment they think needs correcting. This is the wrong approach.

The integration process, as mentioned previously, between the four absolutes and the six swing components is the key to swing analysis through diagnosing and prescribing. It is through this interrelationship that you can exactly identify the illness and treat this problem. In analyzing the swing, you will learn to diagnose and prescribe by treating the anatomical body segment from within the four mechanical absolutes and six swing components. In other words, you will learn to identify the mechanical absolute problem in question within one of the swing components and correct the corresponding body segment. No more guess work!

Problem Recognition

To help you identify the illness (problem recognition), coach, you must keep in mind the following concepts: (1) the goals at contact; (2) the integration of the four absolutes and the six swing components; (3) slow-mo demonstration of the hitter's entire swing and stop-freeze demonstration of the hitter's contact position; and (4) the rules of pitch recognition.

Goals at contact:
- arrive on time
- accuracy
- high bat velocity

Demonstration:
- Hitter demonstrates his stop-freeze swing at contact
- Hitter demonstrates his slow-mo swing.

Rules of Pitch
Recognition:
- First check visual dynamics---complete visual exam; prediction recognition---timing of stride at release of pitch.
- Look for a mechanical flaw consistency---don't correct only a single at bat.
- NEVER try to correct a mechanical flaw in a game---impossible to do.
- In a game, focus on the visual awareness cues and pitch locations swung at.
- In a game, give only positive reinforcement visual cues.
- Use video equipment.

To identify correctly the illness, the procedure is as follows:

- Review the swing completely one through. We are assuming the swing in question represents the consistent mechanical flaw.

- Next, focus on the body and bat positions at CONTACT. Usually, the results of the problem will surface here.

- **Third determine by tracing back from contact where in the swing components the flaw was first recognized.**

- Lastly, correct the anatomical body segment where it first was identified in one of the swing components that is causing the mechanical problem at contact.

Problem Solving: Prescription

In this section, we will identify the young players' most common and major mechanical hitting problems, and then prescribe the treatment. The following illnesses are the most common hitting faults: (1) the bailer; (2) the lunger; (3) the caster; (4) the spinner; (5) the hitcher/uppercutter; and (6) the drifter.

A second category of hitting problems resides in the visual area. First, we will identify these visual problems, then prescribe the treatment. The most common visual hitting problems are as follows: (1) tracking; (2) pitch recognition; and (3) predicting pitch locations---knowing the strike zone.

⦿ *COACHING TIP*

Correct the consistent mechanical flaw. Check your own visual diagnosis through high-speed video. The camera sees best.

Mechanical Problem 1: The "Bailer"

Problem Recognition:

"Stepping in the bucket" is the number one problem with all hitters as they first start out swinging the bat. Fear is the illness; the symptom is the lead striding foot stepping away (bailing out) from the oncoming pitch.

Solution:

- **Lock player into the stride box. Monitor stride direction and length.**

- Pitch underhand softer balls: nerf balls, rubber balls, etc., that are optic orange in color to improve tracking skills; use stride box in conjunction with this drill.

- Swing the "Swing-Loop" with an optic orange baseball; use stride box in conjunction with this drill.

- Pitch overhand softer balls; work up to the 5 oz. baseball as fear subsides; use stride box in conjunction with this drill.

Stride Box

Swing Loop

Mechanical Problem 2: The "Lunger"

Problem Recognition:

This hitter exhibits an abnormally long stride; and/or as he lunges forward in his stride he could also bring his hands too soon and too far forward (commits his upper half too soon). These are symptoms of the illness. The illness is the emphasis by the hitter and hitting coach to produce a weight transfer (shift) swing.

Solution:

- Emphasize the swing is a sequence: a short weight shift stride into rotation.

- Lock hitter into stride box; use hitting tee drills and live batting practice to control stride direction and distance; use optic orange baseballs.

- Open up his stance; and emphasize a short stride as he "walks away from his hands."

Mechanical Problem 3: The "Caster"

Problem Recognition:

This type of hitter is the most difficult to identify. You must use video, preferably high-speed shutter video cameras. A casting hitter is a player that starts his bat out and away from his body in an angular or circular motion during the approach. He begins the bat approach with the barrel of the bat leading the hands. The path of the caster's bat route is circular. Hence the analogy: the hitter looks like the fisherman as he casts his line away from his body toward the target. The result will be a SWEEPING or LONG SWING.

Symptoms seen by the naked eye are as follows: (1) Hands at rest in the stance are too far away from the body, (2) Long back swing during the stride with the bat and hands well behind the back shoulder; (3) Dropping of the hands and back shoulder before the approach; and (4) Hands at the beginning of the approach cast out from the body (hard to see with unaided eye).

Solution:

- Use high-speed shutter video cameras to detect this problem. The video will confirm your eyes' diagnosis as they spot the symptoms.

- Bring the hitter's hands into his chest. Have him actually touch his chest and start the swing from this position. Don't mistake this hands' position as position of weakness against the inside pitch. If the hitter takes the **"knob of the bat to the ball"** from this position, his hands will generate enough bat velocity to hit the inside pitch. Develop this **TOUCH SYSTEM**, then eventually he can move his hands outward between 3 to 5 inches from his body.

- Use the verbal and visual cue, "take the knob to the ball."

Mechanical Problem 4: The "Spinner"

Problem Recognition:

The "spinner" exhibits a premature pulling out, or opening up of the front shoulder, hip, and head during the stride. This premature rotating of the body acts like an uncontrolled spinning top. The result is: (1) topping the outside pitch and weakly grounding out; and/or (2) a turning of the head too far and missing the ball completely and consistently. Therefore, the spinner has a major mechanical swing flaw leading into a common visual tracking problem.

Solution:

- Use stride box and batting tee combination. Lock player into the correct stride direction and length while hitting off the tee and in BP.

- Hands-on the hitter by the coach: Move the player through the correct kinetic link---rotational sequence. Rotation is initiated by the front hip rotation at stride completion as the stride foot-heel plants down.

- Place a baseball just out in front of the plate. Instruct the hitter after contact to look at the ball in front of the plate, emphasizing keeping the head down.

Mechanical Problem 5: The "Hitcher/Uppercutter"

Problem Recognition:

The hitcher/uppercutter has noticeable anatomical symptoms. The back side of this hitter is where the glaring symptoms surface. The hands are usually held very high, at or above shoulder level. As the player strides, the hitter drops (hitches) his hands before he brings his hands and bat forward---two movements. His hitching hands ride the "vertical elevator."   Hitching causes the back shoulder to drop resulting in an uppercut swing. This swing is slow resulting in frequent missed pitches, lots of foul balls and pop flies. As the back shoulder drops below the front shoulder during the approach into contact, the hitter is usually hitting off the back leg (CG is over the back leg).

The Uppercutter

Solution:

- Rest the bat on the hitter's shoulder. Start the swing from this position.

- Teach proper rotational sequence in the Kinetic Link. Start from a well-balanced stance, with level and parallel feet, knees, hips, shoulders and head.

- Hands-on by the coach: Place your hands on the hitter's shoulders and guide the hitter through the swing. He must feel the difference between the uppercut motion and a level to downward swing.

- Use the batting tee with a net-target. The hitter tries to drive the ball into targets that emphasize a line drive result. Adjust the tee so the hitter hits the high pitch on a line (line drive)---the swing will be a little downward. Usually, the uppercutter has a difficult time hitting the low and high strokes.

Mechanical Problem 6: The "Drifter"

Problem Recognition:

The drifter is a hitter that has an excessive weight shift forward during his stride. During his stride, he noticeably tries to hit off his front leg. The results show that as his stride lead foot plants down, his leading hip continues forward (drifting) toward the pitcher. Therefore, his center of gravity (CG) continues toward the pitcher causing late rotation, possible lunging and unbalance body problems.

Solution:

- Use the stride box.

- Teach that the swing is a sequence---first weight shift, then rotation.

- Once the hitter commits to swing, point out to him that at the end of his stride, as the lead foot-heel plants down, he should begin rotating to contact. This emphasis will control his excessive CG drift.

- Hands-on drill. Guide the hitter through the proper swing with your hands.

Perceptual-Motor Problem Recognition:

The following three perceptual-motor problems are basically visual problems that can be corrected if the coaching staff emphasizes on-field visual dynamic training.

Visual Problem 1: Tracking

Problem Recognition:

At contact, the hitter with a tracking problem will arrive late to the ball, demonstrating a high frequency of errors. He will foul off an abnormal amount of pitches and/or miss a lot of pitches during batting practice.

Solution:

- Use the video camera---video the interface between the pitcher and hitter. See when the hitter is striding. If he is striding after the ball is released, chances are he is striding too late. Therefore, he will not arrive at contact on time.

- During batting practice, instruct the hitter to center on the ball at release. The coach should throw from a set position, showing the ball clearly (hold ball at release point-stop action, then throw) and emphasize to the hitter to track the ball from the hand.

- **Use optic orange baseballs during batting practice.**

- The hitter should hit within the stride box. If he learns the proper weight shift-rotational sequence, his head and eyes will be in the best anatomical position to track the pitch.

- The hitter should always try and track the taken pitch to the catcher's glove.

- On-deck hitters during batting practice must stand behind the cage and practice tracking pitches.

- Use the swing-loop hitting aid. Emphasize tracking the ball continuously as the ball travels in a circle.

Visual Problem 2: Pitch Recognition

Problem Recognition:

At contact, the timing of the hitter is off. He arrives too early or too late. This is usually a result of his indecisiveness to what type of pitch has been thrown. The timing of the stride is incorrect.

Solution:

- **Have the hitter center on the hand at release and not just look at the whole body of the pitcher during the delivery.**

- Use the stride box. Mix up different types of pitches during batting practice.

- The on-deck hitter tracks pitches from behind the cage during batting practice.

Visual Problem 3: Pitch Location Recognition

Problem Recognition:

Pitch location recognition is the most common and destructive visual hitting problem of all. The hitter with this visual problem does not know the strike zone. The best hitters over the course of the season swing at more strikes and less bad pitches than poor hitters. They always seem to get the "good" pitch to hit. Why?

They know the strike zone; and they are balanced at contact which allows the head to be in the best anatomical position so that the eyes can track the pitch.

Solution:

- Use the stride box. Teach the proper weight shift-rotational swing sequence.

- Use optic orange baseballs during batting practice.

- **While the on-deck hitter stands behind the cage during batting practice, he calls out the location of the pitch. The hitter also calls out the location of the pitch.**

- **Use the swing-loop hitting aid.**

- **Have the hitter stand next to the catcher while the pitcher is warming up in the bullpen. Track all the pitches into the catcher's glove.**

BOX SCORE

Treat the illness not the symptom. Under the eye of the camera, find the mechanical flaw at ball-bat contact. Then trace back through the swing components to find where the mechanical flaw was initiated. Then correct the body part causing the mechanical problem. In practice use a specific drill to correct the mechanical flaw.

X
Strategy

"You win some, you lose some,
but we give away more than we lose."

--Dr. Coop DeRenne

Never say: "We had the game, we let it slip away, we should have won, we are better than they are, etc."...Say WE LOST. Give no excuses. EXCUSES CLOUD THE EVALUATION PROCESS. Ask why?...Analyze the loss in terms of talent, strategy, coaching mistakes and preparation.

If you lose to a better ball club, then concede the victory. If you lost to an inferior ball club, then you gave it away. How? You need better preparation in the form of: (1) player development; (2) better coaching strategy; and (3) INFORM, INSTRUCT AND INSPIRE.

🔵 *COACHING TIP*

MOST GOOD FOOD TEAMS WIN BECAUSE OF BETTER TALENT AND COACHING. MOST AVERAGE TEAMS LOSE MORE CLOSE GAMES AND GIVE MORE GAMES AWAY BECAUSE OF THE LACK OF GOOD COACHING AND PREPARATION. BECAUSE YOU CANNOT MAKE A PLOW HORSE INTO A RACE HORSE, PREPARATION IS THE GREAT EQUALIZER.

WAYS TO WIN GAMES

CARDINAL SINS

- **NEVER** make the first or third out at third base or home plate.

- **NEVER** hit to the left side of the infield with a runner on second with no outs.

- **NEVER** bat your best hitter fourth. In a six or seven inning game, he might be on deck when the last out is made. Hit your best hitter third. He will come up at the end of the game to tie or win the game more often than your clean-up hitter.

- **ELIMINATE** unnecessary outfield throws trying to get the lead runner. More often than not, the lead runner is safe, and the batter-runner or the backup runner advances an extra base. It is this advancement by backup runners that cost you games.

🔵 *COACHING TIP*

RULE OF THUMB: IF THE BALL IS HIT HARD RIGHT AT THE OUTFIELDER SO HE CAN CHARGE DIRECTLY AT THE LEAD BASE, THEN MAKE THE THROW. IF NOT, THROW AHEAD OF THE BACKUP RUNNER OR BATTER-RUNNER TO PREVENT HIM FROM ADVANCING.

- **ELIMINATE** the unnecessary infield throws after a boot or bobble. A hurried and unnecessary throw in this case could lead to a second error.

- **ELIMINATE** unnecessary pick-off attempts by the pitcher at third base. This unnecessary throw leads to runs.

- **ELIMINATE** unnecessary pick-off throws by the catcher at any base. This leads to advanced runners and runs.

- **ELIMINATE** "crossed signals (mix-ups)" between the catcher and pitcher with runners on base.

Defense

- Teach your catcher to "take charge," to be the general of the infield. He must become vocal and run the defense.

- All defensive players must learn to adjust pitch-by-pitch.

- Teach your defense instincts. During the week's practices conduct simulated games. Teach your players how to react, anticipate and adjust during these game situations.

- Do not have too many defensive plays or too many difficult executing plays. The more complicated the defense, the more errors will likely occur.

- Teach the philosophy that all fielders move to the ball. A ground ball is always the outfielder's unless the infielder cuts it off. This helps the outfielders to "get a good jump" and into the habit of always backing up the bases.

- Infielders must learn to react. Again, teach them that infield play is "side-to-side." Therefore, the ready position is not glove down and out, but in and up. Also, that they should think on every pitch that the ball hit at them will be really smoked.

- The corners must stay off the lines, even in late innings when you are tied or ahead--play the percentages.

- The middle infielders: Shortstops must stay out of the middle. This is the easy ground ball. Shortstops should cheat toward the hole, so they can cut off these difficult ground balls. Second basemen should cheat toward second base. For the second baseman, the up-to-the-middle ground balls and throws are his toughest plays.

- Outfielders: All outfielders must learn to get a jump on the fly ball. This is the most important quality that he possesses. The outfielder should play shallow during batting practice, etc., so he can practice getting his jumps. He must watch for ball-bat contact so he can pick up the ball as soon as possible. Outfielders must learn how to play the hitters. They all must learn to hit the cutoff man. Require all outfielders to hustle and backup the bases on every play.

- Pitchers: Coaches, you must teach your pitchers how to: cover first base; field bunts; lead your shortstop on double play come-backers; hold on base runners; and backup third base and home plate.

Offense

- Teach the following hitting fundamentals: bunts-sacrifice, drag, and squeeze; learn the strike zone; swing at only strikes; hit to the opposite field; quick hands-turn on (pull) the middle-in pitches; learn to hit the breaking pitches; track the ball at release; and learn to slash and hit & run.

- Lineup: Put speed ahead of power. The weak hitter that hits toward the end of your lineup is a role hitter. Teach the role hitter positive hitting skills (e.g., bunt, slash, etc.) and use those strengths in the clutch. NEVER ASK PLAYERS TO EXECUTE IF THEY HAVEN'T PRACTICED IT, OR IF THEY ARE INCAPABLE OF DELIVERING.

WAYS TO LOSE GAMES

<u>Defense</u>

Defensive Philosophy: (1) stay out of the big inning; (2) settle down the position players and pitchers in pressured situations with positive talk; (3) most coaches wait too long to remove the pitcher---remove him when he is tired and/or when he has lost his velocity; and (4) again, beware of the "two-out syndrome" (leaving the pitcher in too long as he tries to get the final out while he's scuffling). The rule of thumb in this situation is ALWAYS BRING IN THE FRESH ARM.

Here is a list of "game breakers" that cost teams games:

- Missed signals by players. Missed opportunities by coaches.

- Overcoaching---calling too many plays. Let the kids play!

- Coach, you neglected to move your defensive players.

- Calling the wrong type of game for your pitcher. You must locate and change speeds to win. Even if your pitcher doesn't have his best stuff, locate and change speeds...he may get a lot of swinging strikes.

- Failing to have the bullpen ready when needed. Failing to have your starting infielder or outfielder warm and ready to pitch while he is playing defense.

- Failing to recognize the "two-out syndrome." You left the pitcher in too long because you kept thinking he can get the final out.

- Failing to prepare the bench to produce by not giving them extra at bats during blown out games, and not teaching them offensive skills to be used in their role positions.

- Infielders: Throwing to the wrong base; failing to backup each other and backup the bases; failing to be alert on every pitch; and rushing the throw after bobbling or misplaying a ground ball.

- Outfielders: Catching fly balls and ground balls one-handed; throwing to the wrong base; not hustling and backing up the bases and backing up each other; failing to know how to play the opposing hitters; not communicating with each other on fly balls; and day dreaming.

Offense

At the plate: (1) the coach puts too much pressure on the hitter by yelling at him or giving him a batting lesson during the game; (2) the hitter misses a sign; (3) the coach asks the hitter to execute under pressure when he hasn't properly prepared the hitter in practice (e.g., squeeze bunt); (4) a hitter fouls off or misses the pitch in a squeeze bunt situation; fouls off the pitch as a runner is stealing in a guaranteed thief situation...have the weak hitter take the pitch; (5) you asked a player to bunt with poor mechanics and/or a poor attitude; (6) you are giving too many take signs; and (7) your signs are too difficult to remember.

Base running: (1) the runner did not anticipate the ball in the dirt so he could not have advanced to the next base as the catcher missed the ball; (2) the runner was running with his head down--missed the error and/or the coach's sign--no extra base advancement by the runner; (3) the base runner has a timid attitude; (4) the base runner doesn't know the different kinds of slides and under what conditions to execute each of them; and (5) the base runner failed to slide in an obvious sliding situation.

Coaching the lines: (1) the coach is not alert; (2) the coach is too worried about the hitter...Coach, your first priority is paying attention to your base runners. Therefore, the managers must give the signs to the hitters from the dugout. The coaches on the lines must take care of their base runners; and (3) don't teach while coaching the lines (this is a visual distraction).

From the bench: Lost games will occur if you fail to do the following: (1) the manager gives the offensive and defensive signs from the bench; (2) coaches, only give visual instructions; (3) always be positive and encourage your players; (4) constantly ask game questions to your substitutes--keep them in the game; (5) plan ahead for substitutes, especially have the bullpen ready ahead of time; and (6) play the subs as much as possible--prepare them for a specific role; get them ready in case a starter goes down.

SUBSTITUTES

The most difficult coaching responsibility you have is to play your substitutes a fair amount of time. In order to be fair to your subs, you must have a positive attitude toward this responsibility. Remember, **YOU WEAR YOUR BELIEFS.**

Philosophy

You win with bench strength, not with your starters. The better your bench, the better the team. Define your subs' roles and put them into successful situations. The more they come face-to-face with Mr. Pressure, the more they will come through for you in the clutch. As you are nurturing these players, count on your key starters for clutch performances. Eventually, the subs will come through as you bring them along slowly.

Development

Here is a check list as to how you might develop these special players:

• Identify the strengths of your subs. Develop these skills in each player. In practice give each sub positive encouragement and positive experiences to develop that strength.

• Identify the weaknesses of your subs. Remember, the sub's weaknesses will take a longer time to improve. Therefore, do not have great expectations but have great PATIENCE.

• Substitutes need a tremendous amount of encouragement. If you are frustrated by their below average abilities, just think how frustrated they are. Positive psychological vitamins and reinforcement will help you to improve their performance. Remember, negativism only works in the short-term.

• Put them in game role positions and give them a chance to succeed. Success fosters confidence and concentration. Once a player has these two "C's," he will become a better performer.

• Repeat the above four steps continuously.

SLUMPS

Identification

Why do slumps occur? Are slumps more mental than mechanical? How do I get my players out of their slumps--bench or play them? These are common questions all managers and coaches ask every week from the big leagues down the ranks to our amateur youth leagues. No one has all the answers, but SCIENCE pinch hits and helps stop the bleeding....

Coach, you must understand that baseball is first a visual sport then a mechanical sport. The visual aspect of the game is more important than the mechanical.   No one would ever play the game blindfolded. Therefore, slumps are usually first a visual condition leading to secondary mechanical flaws.

In hitting, the visual system controls the clarity of the ball after release. Therefore, hitters do not see the ball as clearly as possible when they begin their slump. They are in the physical channel. They forget to go through the concentration process (visualization, centering, tracking). If their concentration is retarded then they become less confident (mental condition) at the plate. And without total concentration and confidence, the hitter's mechanics begin to deteriorate.

It is no less with the pitchers. Every pitcher has the same solitary goal with every pitch: hit the target! Therefore, pitching mechanics start with the visual system.   Again, if the pitcher is not going through the concentration process before each pitch because of environmental or emotional distractions, his performance will degenerate.

Solution

Once you have identified that most slumps begin with a deteriorating visual system, then do the following:

- Add more visual drills into your practices.

- Reinforce the visual system in the games. Do not put your player in the physical system during the game.

• Continue to give positive vitamins and reinforcements.

• Put the slumping player into "guaranteed" successful situations to booster his confidence.

• Remember, they must **HIT OR PITCH THEIR WAY OUT OF A SLUMP.**

• Reinforce the concentration sequential process for your hitters:
  • In the dugout: ask visual questions; visualize your last at bat and perfect swing.
  • In the On-Deck Circle: visualize your perfect swing; center on the ball through the pitcher's entire delivery; read the pitch at release and track the ball to ball-bat contact or the catcher's glove.
  • At the plate: stay in the visual channel--visualize your perfect swing before stepping into the box; center on the ball trough the pitcher's entire delivery; read the pitch at release (pick up the seams); track the ball to ball-bat contact or into the catcher's glove; ask after every pitch, "Did I see the ball as big as a beach ball and was it very slow?"; after every swing step out of the box, get the sign, ask the visual question and visualize your perfect swing; step back into the box and center on the ball through the delivery and track to contact; DO NOT THINK OR FOCUS ON YOUR MECHANICS--TRUST YOUR SWING.

• On the mound: the pitcher's sequential concentration process is as follows:
  • Step off the mound, gather your composure, and visualize your best delivery. Do not become emotional or distracted with the environment around you (e.g., trouble on the bases or with the opposing hitter).
  • Step back onto the rubber. This is a signal (a button on the rubber) to clear your mind and get the next sign.
  • Center only in the middle of the catcher's glove. DO NOT THINK MECHANICS OR WORRY. TRUST YOUR MECHANICS...Throw to the target and let the delivery happen.

Coach, once you have begun working on their visual systems, then identify the specific mechanical flaw in their swing or delivery. Next, do the following:

- Add specific mechanical drills in practice to cure their bad habits. Remember the neuromuscular memory theory: **THE MORE PERFECT REPETITIONS IN PRACTICE MAKES THE GAME EXECUTIONS PERFECT.**

Ⓑ *COACHING TIP*

AS YOU APPROACH THE MOUND WHEN YOUR PITCHER IS IN TROUBLE, YOU DO NOT NEED TO LECTURE HIM WHY YOU ARE THERE. CALM HIM DOWN, AND REMIND HIM OF THE SEQUENTIAL CONCENTRATION PROCESS. GIVE HIM SOME POSITIVE VITAMINS AND LEAVE THE MOUND.

BOX SCORE

Don't get caught with your pants down or watching the paint dry--plan ahead and stay alert with every pitch.

XI
Tournament Play

*"In tournaments, there is little difference
between winners and losers.... Preparation
and discipline neutralizes superior talent."*

--Dr. Coop DeRenne

PREPARATION

All coaches should have the opportunity to coach in a state or regional tournament, and in a world series. It is a tremendous learning experience. You will learn as much or more than your players. You will learn more about your players under tournament conditions than at any other stage in their development. This is because of the higher level of competition, travel adjustments, and **PRESSURE**. You will learn much about your own abilities--coaching responsibilities, coaching effectiveness, tolerance threshold, and ability to adjust under PRESSURE.

Remember your three I's: **INFORM, INSTRUCT AND INSPIRE.** Plan ahead and plan ways to combat the pressure. It is not the most talented team that always wins the tournament. It usually is the team that is best prepared and that best handles the pressure that walks away with first place. Therefore...

> ### TOURNAMENT WINS ARE A FUNCTION OF PREPARATION AND DISCIPLINE

Your coaching effectiveness--information, instruction and inspiration will determine how you and your players handle the pressure. You and the players must be in a relaxed confident **AND DISCIPLINED** state throughout the tournament. This condition is the result of **PREPARATION.**

Recognize that pressure is your number one enemy in tournaments. It's hidden and has many disguises. Neutralize its effects! If you don't, when you lose you won't know why and you will not be able to prepare for the next game as effectively.

Team Selection

Coach, what is your philosophy of selecting the all-star team? You need the right chemistry of good talent ("ATHLETES") and a good selection of interchangeable parts (bench strength). The most important attributes to look for are: (1) mental toughness; (2) athletic ability (agility and instincts); (3) speed; and (4) strength. In short tournaments, take heed of Socrates' advice: *"A good big player is better than a good small player any day."*

The grueling demands of the foreign environment of the heat, or unpredictable weather, hotel accommodations, foreign food (no Mom's home cooking), little rest, doubleheaders, and a thousand unforeseeable minor problems and distractions added to the constant feeling of pressure makes the statement, **"ONLY THE STRONG WILL SURVIVE,"** a truism.

Do not ever underestimate the importance of your bench strength. As you select your substitutes, look for "athletes" that can play more than one position and fill a needed role. Speed and agility are two of the most important athletic qualities to look for in these players.

The size of your team is very important. Fatigue and injury factors dictate that you will need a large squad. The total number is based on the following criteria: (1) starters; (2) one extra middle infielder; (3) two extra outfielders; (3) one extra catcher; and (4) 4-6 pitchers. Therefore, a minimum squad of 15 players is necessary.

Commitment/Team Effort

Before the team is selected, all prospects and their parents must understand "team commitment." All players, parents and coaches must make commitments and sacrifices for the total team effort. There is a trend today that it is okay to break commitments. Everyone must sacrifice time, effort, energy and agree to a new temporary lifestyle for the sake of the all-star team.

Young players are inherently concerned with individual statistics--hits, home runs, and number of wins. Basically, players are self-centered. They must be taught the importance of team effort statistics. Baseball is a game divided into two parts---offense and defense: (1) Good defense is just as important as the offense; (2) certain positions are defensive oriented, therefore, the offense is second; (3) if you have a lack of offense that day, if the other team doesn't score because of your good defense and pitching, then you end up in a tie---no loss; and (4) remember coach, you build a team based on the following premise:

> GOOD PITCHING NEUTRALIZES GOOD HITTING; AND GOOD DEFENSE MAKES GOOD PITCHING GREAT.

Coach/Parent Meetings

During parental meetings you must cover the following points: (1) Before the parents and players commit to the all-star team, they must understand that it is an honor and privilege to play for the team. The team comes first; (2) The trip is also an educational experience. Therefore, the players and parents must understand that not everyone will play an equal amount; (3) During practices and scrimmages, you will give every player an equal chance to show his talent.

Team Moms & Dads

The team Mom or Dad is responsible for the following (you will need help): (1) plan the trip--travel and hotel accommodations, sightseeing excursions, car rentals, etc.; (2) business transactions, etc.; (3) help prepare for the games--ice, first aid kit, food, transportation, etc. Basically, your role is to relieve the manager and his coaches of too many business distractions.

Coaching Own Son

This is a tremendous responsibility and a sensitive area. It will actually become a major distraction, if you let it. You might become overly concerned with his behavior and performance. Beware not to let your relationship cloud your judgment or distract you from your responsibilities. You must make a supreme effort to treat him just like everyone else. This is practically impossible; so have another coach look after him. Try and not be too critical. Don't follow his practice or game actions (his every move)--it will take you away from coaching the other players.

Practices

Here is a helpful list of practice tips:

- There is no substitute for preparation. Plan every minute.

- Address the six components of performance in your practices: mechanics of the positions; visual dynamics; mental conditioning; physical conditioning; nutritional conditioning; and injury prevention.

- Identify every players' strengths. Work with these strengths to identify the roles of every player.

- Every practice should last no more than two hours.

- You should play a few game simulation innings whenever possible.

- You must scrimmage older and better talented teams.

- Conduct mini-bullpens three days in a row. These bullpens are for control enhancements. They are: 5 minutes in length; one-half the regulation distance; thrown on flat ground; work on locations and mechanics (e.g., specific pitches); and one-half velocity.

- Develop specific offensive and defensive fundamental plays. Do not be too technical.

TRICK PLAYS LOOK GOOD WITH BAD RESULTS. PERFECT FUNDAMENTAL EXECUTIONS WIN!

- Teach players how to think, react and ADJUST by playing simulated games.

- Develop a game plan. A well thought out game plan is based on good information. Implementing the game plan is better than relying on your players' good instincts. Instincts are developed naturally as the play is developing--instincts are a part of the resulting play, the decision-making process.

ⓞ *COACHING TIP*

(1)   INSTINCTS ARE A FUNCTION OF GOOD INFORMATION + GAME SIMULATION DRILLS...RESULTING IN QUICK DECISIONS DURING ACTION PLAYS.

(2)   INSTINCTS ARE NO MATCH FOR GOOD INFORMATION AND GUIDANCE.

Scrimmages

Here are some important points to remember about scrimmages.

- Play as many scrimmages as you can, but give your players approximately four days rest before the first all-star game. Burn-out or fatigue will happen if you do not rest your players before the trip.

- Rotate your players during the first few scrimmages. Find your key position players ASAP and play them all the time. Develop up-the-middle-strength, team unity and cohesiveness.

- After you find your four of five starting players (catcher, SS, 2B, center fielder, starting pitchers and closer), rotate all the other players to find their best defensive position and offensive strengths. Develop your bench.

- In the last half of the scrimmages, play your players according to their roles. Prepare everyone for their team specific role.

Chalk Talks Sessions

Cover the following strategies continuously:

- Go over all **FUNDAMENTAL** plays and signs.

- SLIDING: no sliding into first base; no head first slides---hurt hands, then you can't field or hit; the pop-up slide is best---you can advance quicker to the next base, and you can possibly kick the ball out of the infielder's glove.

- BASE RUNNING: always run through first base; as you round each base, tag the inside part of the base; as you are running the bases, pick-up the position of the outfielder and pick-up the flight of the ball to determine if to advance or not; anticipate---look for ways to take the extra base (e.g., curveball in the dirt, shuffle out toward the next base and go if it bounces to the side of the catcher).

- STEALING: Steal on the first two pitches if...weak throwing catcher, poor and slow delivery of pitcher, best base stealer on base. If it is a guaranteed stolen base situation, or if you need the stolen base to tie or win, steal and have the hitter take the pitch.

- THROWING TO THE BASES: (1) Do not throw to the advance base unless the ball is hit hard and right at the outfielder--- percentages are not in the outfielder's favor; (2) throw in front of the runners and batter-runner; don't let the hitter get the extra base.

Departure

Before departure, in a team/parental meeting, discuss the following:

- Acceptable and proper team and individual behavior.

- Flights, hotels, transportation.

- Schedules: Practices, games, curfews, free time, etc.

- Equipment: baseball gear; first aid kit; coolers of ice; etc.

- Duties: business manager; parent trained in first aid, CPR, and massaging; ask for athletic trainers at tournament fields.

TOURNAMENT GAMES

<u>Tournament Rules Meeting</u>

Before the tournament commences, it is very important that you review the games' schedule and tournament rules. Usually, the tournament games' schedule and rules will be printed before the tournament. Study your rules and review the games' schedule before the tournament rules meeting. Pay close attention to the following: (1) scheduled back-to-back doubleheaders (disadvantage); (2) scheduled doubleheaders in the "heat" (11-3pm of the day); and (3) pitching rules that allow a coach to overuse his best two or three pitchers.

At the tournament meeting, be sure to have all of your questions answered and understand thoroughly all rules. If the local team entry or any other team has a playing advantage, discuss the situation with the tournament officials. Make your voice be heard and follow-up with a letter to the national office.

<u>Practices</u>

It is important to arrive early to acclimate with the environment and field conditions. All practices must be fun (light-hearted), motivational and free of pressure. Go over your fundamental offensive and defensive plays and do a lot of hitting and bunting. The key to your success is your pitching and defense. Keep a close eye on your pitchers---the pressure, injuries, mental conditions, fatigue, adequate rest, etc.

Before each game, take batting practice on a scheduled field. Eliminate environmental and tournament distractions. Be careful not to hit too early in the heat of the day. The sun is a tremendous energy drainer, even if the players are not running around. BP must be crisp, clean, and fast. Have plenty of cold water available for the players. No sodas or juices. Electrocyte drinks are not the best fluids---cold water is a must. Show-up in time for the game to warm-up and take infield.

Competitive Games

As your team enters the ballpark, each player loses his individuality and takes on the responsibility of representing his city, state, and team. Therefore, each player must abide by DeRenne's Golden Player Rules:

    (1)   **RESPECT ALL OFFICIALS-THEIR DECISIONS AND BEHAVIORS. THIS INCLUDES YOUR OWN COACHES AND PARENTS, TEAMMATES, OPPONENTS, UMPIRES, OTHER COACHES, AND TOURNAMENT OFFICIALS.**

    (2)   **BE A RESPECTABLE CITIZEN AND HAVE CLASS.** *THEREFORE, RECOGNIZE IT IS A PRIVILEGE TO PARTICIPATE IN THE TOURNAMENT; AND THE TRIP IS A VALUABLE EDUCATIONAL EXPERIENCE.*

Coaches, You have a code of conduct you must abide by. You must be a gentleman at all times. Remember, you are a role model. You must never lose sight of this fact. Your true character will be tested numerous times over the course of the trip. You must constantly look for examples to teach and reinforce proper behavior and conduct. Helping your players to grow during this educational experience is more important than a first place trophy.... DeRenne's Coaches' Code of Honor:

ALWAYS RESPECT THE OTHER TEAMS' PLAYERS AND COACHES.

NEVER: (1) deliberately run-up the score by stealing with a big lead in the last two innings; or sacrifice or drag bunt with a big lead; or squeeze bunting to obtain a "ten-run-rule"; (2) show-up the other team by laughing at poor play, or pointing fingers, fists in the air or other gestures when you make an outstanding play (e.g., home run, strikeout, etc.); (3) show-up an umpire or tournament official.

Motivational Gimmicks

The only requirements you can place upon your team is to hustle and play with desire. If they do, reward your players: they choose their favorite restaurant (within reason); and they may help plan their off-day excursions and free time.

During the course of the game have a bucket filled with ice water and ammonia (a natural high) to wipe their faces and to wake them up during hot days or "dog day" doubleheaders.

Treat your players as special people whenever you have the chance. Allow them to swim and use the hotel jacuzzi. Rub down or massage your injured players or pitchers. Let them eat their favorite foods at least once a day. Take them shopping, rent videos, and allow them to socialize as much as possible.

In return, demand hustle and effort, gentlemanly behavior, and attendance at team meetings. Enforce team rules and curfews. Select responsible captains. At team meetings, be very positive, discuss strategy, and point out the value of each player's team contribution. **Don't add to the tournament pressure.**

The Bench

Your bench is known as the *Interchangeable Parts*. Your bench is just as important as your starting players. Develop these players for vital offensive and defensive roles. They need playing time. Find ways to give them pressure experiences.

Nutrition

Here are some basic nutritional rules:

- Allow the players to choose their favorite foods at least once a day.

- Plea bargain: no junk food before a game, but after a game they may have junk food or snacks.

- Energy source: A pre-game meal (2 hours before the game) should consist of complex carbohydrates, cold water or natural juice, fruits and vegetables.

- Balance: Select a balanced diet from the six food groups:

> meat and meat alternatives
> milk and dairy
> grains
> fruit
> vegetables
> fat: small amounts of nuts, seeds, salad dressing, margarine

- NOTE: DRINK LOTS OF WATER.

- Cut down or cut out: junk foods, "sweets," and sodas.

Offensive Strategy

Here's a proven list of offensive weapons:

- Somehow, always get the first hitter on board anyway you can. Over 70 percent of the time, the lead-off hitter will score if he reaches base.

- A balance attack is the best offensive weapon.

- Score early. Put more pressure on their defense.

- Teach "Billy Ball." Manufacture runs (e.g., hit & run; run & hit; run & slash; bunt; steal bases) when the opposition has more talent than you.

- Cut down on the strikeouts. Strikeouts kill desire. Do anything you have to do so that your players never get dominated by a superior pitcher.

- Recognize when the enemy has superior talent. Manufacture runs. Do not try and slug it out.

- Never play for the big inning against a superior talent. Get an early lead, chip away, and put constant pressure on their defense.

- Always look for the extra base.

- BUNTING: The 21 outs in the game are precious---why give up an out and sacrifice. Why bunt early and give up one of those precious outs? Bunt only to win or tie; and use the bunt as a surprise weapon.

- Don't over coach. Let the kids play. But, when you have to manufacture runs, then coach.

Defensive Strategy

Here's a list of defensive winners:

- The first pitch to every hitter is a strike. Do not let the lead-off hitter reach base.

- Teach fundamentals and stress to your fielders to make the routine play. Trick plays and difficult defensive plays only work in the short-term. More than not, they will backfire.

- It is important to play your defense according to the strengths of the opposing hitters than to use trick plays. Move your defensive players and gamble.

- Do not guard the lines in the late innings. The percentage is to play normal.

- Do not make unnecessary throws.

- Teach pick-off plays. But, never pick-off at third---a bad throw or a balk, and a run scores.

- When possible, play the infield in to cut off an important run. Make the play at the plate easier for your infield. Put pressure on the offense.

- Your defense is only as strong as your middle strengths. Therefore, if possible never interchange your starting shortstop, second baseman, center fielder, and catcher.

- Teach the outfield to: communicate; field with two hands; judge fly balls; charge ground balls; throw ahead of the runners; backup every base; and be alert.

Ⓜ *COACHING TIP*

Most games are lost, not won. Remember, expect errors; these kids are not miniature adults.

Pitching

Here's a list of pitching wisdoms:

- Throw strikes. Throw more strikes. And throw more strikes.

- Throw a strike on the first pitch to every hitter, even if the pitch is your pitcher's second or third best pitch.

- Get ahead and stay ahead of the hitters.

- Mix the pitches up. Youth league hitters are prone to swinging at bad pitches. Therefore, even if the breaking pitches or change-ups are not strikes, throw them anyway.

Ⓜ *COACHING TIP*

We get hitters out two ways---we locate or change speeds.

- Every pitcher should average around 20 pitches per inning. When he has thrown an excessive amount, remove him from the game. **DON'T OVERUSE YOUR STARTERS. PITCH BY COMMITTEE.**

• Be careful of the "Two Out Syndrome." Two quick outs, then all hell breaks loose and your pitcher is still out there because you keep saying to yourself, "with one more pitch we will be out of the inning."

• Warmup your starting pitcher 15 minutes before the game.

• Bullpen: All your relievers should be able to get loose with less than 25 pitches. Warmup a game player early if you might use him in relief. If possible, never pitch your catcher. If so, use him to close the game, then ice his arm. Never pitch him and then put him back behind the plate.

• All pitchers must ice their shoulders and elbows for 15 minutes after a game or practice bullpen.

Slumping Players

Remember, for a top performance every player must have the "R and two C's:" Relaxation (be alert), Confidence, and Concentration.

The slumping hitter and pitcher must play themselves out of the slump. Keep encouraging them with the psychological vitamins. Do not try and correct their physical mechanical flaw during the game. Keep the game visual and not physical. Above all else, you must understand they need confidence. You must show you have confidence in them.

Base Coaches

Base coaches, you are very important to the offense. You can't be too worried about coaching the hitter and neglect your base runner. Your first responsibility is to the base runner. Therefore, **THE MANAGER MUST RUN THE OFFENSE FROM THE DUGOUT AND HIS ASSISTANTS COACH THE BASES.**

Frontrunners

All-stars are not used to losing or failure. If too many of your players are not performing up to their capabilities, they may get down and not hustle-- this is a contagious disease. Remember, the mind says work but the heart says no. The solution is motivation: (1) individual encouragements to players; (2) always have positive comments; (3) bribe--if hustle, then fun after the game; (4) ice and ammonia bucket; (5) rest tired players; (6) get out of the sun; (7) no hitting practice before the game, unless they want it--then challenge them with a game like BP; but always letting them hit some "fat" pitches; and (8) make a deal: let the team eat what they want between games or before the game, if they will hustle...NEVER USE NEGATIVE MOTIVATIONAL TOOLS (e.g., extra running, calisthenics).

Umpire

Coaches, help them move the game along. Don't argue unnecessarily, or bait the umps. Acknowledge their hustle and good calls. Show class and be a gentleman at all times.

BOX SCORE

There is a very fine, distinguished line between tournament winners and losers. This line is not by talent. Preparation separates the men from the boys. Cope with the pressure or it will capsize your team. Preparation and fun will reduce the destructive effects of pressure.

Section Three

EXERCISE SCIENCE

XII
Growth and Development of the Young Athlete

"Through education and awareness the parents, coaches, teachers, and health professionals can work as a team to improve not only childrens' experiences as youths in sports, but make a positive difference in their life experiences which will help mold them and follow them throughout their lives."

--Dr. Tom Harris

The human body is truly amazing. Under normal conditions, the body is able to heal itself, combat infection and adapt to unusual environments and trauma. The body has a built-in alarm system which is triggered when something goes wrong.

Some of the warning signs are aches, pains, headaches, dizziness, and nausea. When an athlete experiences a new or consistent pain, it is a warning. Caught early, treatment may consist of simply taping by the trainer, a flexibility and strengthening program with the physical therapist, or perhaps some time out to allow healing.

If, however, the warning signals are ignored and the athlete "works through the pain", he or she could end up "on the bench" for weeks or months at a time, and might even need surgery. For the young athlete, injuries that are overlooked or ignored can sometimes become even far more serious. Do not force a child to play when hurt. Whether it is a physical or a psychological problem is not important.

> What is important is not to pressure the children into playing when they do not feel like they should.

GROWTH AND DEVELOPMENT

While every athlete needs support, a young athlete needs more--more support, more love and more understanding. It is important to understand that children are not just small adults or scaled-down versions of the full-size model. There are certain things about growth and development which should be taken into consideration when evaluating an exercise or sports activity for young people who have not yet reached their full growth potential.

On the other hand, it has been shown that fitness in childhood, both musculoskeletal and cardiovascular, leads to a healthier, more satisfactory adult life. With a well-designed exercise program, injuries can be prevented. It is important for parents, coaches, trainers, teachers and the young athletes as well, to understand the basics of a good fitness program.

Parents need to encourage children to do something with fitness every day. That way, they develop a pattern of regular exercise at an early age. It's important that physical activity be a regular part of their lives. It's important that they develop this attitude on their own, without a lot of pressure or stress which could discourage them from exercising in the future.

MUSCLES AND COORDINATION

It is important for the parent to understand the concept of coordination and improving coordination, because this is the most important training that a young athlete can get. The earlier the child picks up the sport and learns the movements the more reinforced this neuromuscular pathway becomes and the better the ultimate athlete.

It is important to realize that doing the motion correctly a few times is much more important than doing the movement incorrectly a number of times. **We train movement, then muscles.** Moving a joint with the correct coordination prevents damage to the joint.

There are three types of muscle tissue in your body: voluntary muscles, involuntary muscles and the heart muscle.

Voluntary muscles are the muscles we can move at will. They are the muscles that move the joints. *Involuntary muscles* are the smooth muscles that cause movement in the glands, skin and organs---especially the stomach and intestines. The *heart muscle*, a special blend of muscle fibers that pumps the blood throughout our bodies, is an involuntary muscle.

Voluntary muscles act like the strings of the puppeteer, pulleys which move our limbs and spine in various direction.

They have a broad attachment into the shaft or end of the bone they serve and, on the opposite end, insert into another bone which may be more fixed.

WHAT IS COORDINATION?

Coordination is working the right muscle at the right time efficiently. Most of the time we think of coordination as hand-eye coordination, i.e., throwing the perfect strike. That is part of coordination, but coordination is also postural coordination or balance coordination.

This can also be improved with proper training. With postural coordination and postural strengthening exercises, the muscles tend to become stronger and are available to react when called upon. With postural coordination training, the nerve impulses improve, thus reaction is improved. **Practice improves coordination.**

Coordination is cooperative interaction between the skeletal muscle and the nervous system. *Postural coordination* is the efficient interaction between the skeletal muscles and nervous system to maintain balance.

Strength refers to the amount of force a muscle can generate with muscle *contraction*. In order to increase strength and power of a specific muscle, it must be progressively and gradually challenged or placed under additional stress. This results in hypertrophy (enlargement) of the muscle.

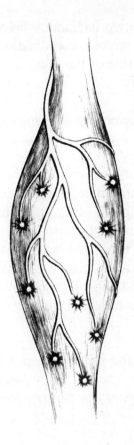

Nerve Impulse. This is an example of the nerve entering the muscle, providing stimulation to the muscle which causes the muscle to contract.

The key here is contraction. A muscle creates no force if it does not contract. To contract, it must receive a nerve impulse.

You cannot strengthen what you cannot recruit!

Contracting muscle fibers pull the bone in a given direction. While this appears as a single movement, for every muscle contraction there must be simultaneous relaxation of the muscle with which it works. It works synergistically---in a rhythmic harmony of contraction and relaxation.

Coordination is the cooperative interaction between the skeletal muscles and the nervous system. Therefore, coordination must be achieved before strengthening a specific muscle or muscles.

Make the right movements first, then strengthen them!

It is important that your muscles work together and that their timing is correct. For example, several muscle groups cooperate to permit you to raise your arm above your head. One group takes the arm to a certain height and releases it, when another group takes over. This process is repeated until your arm is over your head. This relay effort---a series of simultaneous contractions and relaxations---is a classic example of *synergistic action*. Plainly, the inability to move a part to its fullest limit may be caused by the failure of one or more muscle groups to contract or relax in harmony.

Just as strength, endurance and flexibility can be improved with training, coordination can also be improved. With proper, specific training, the efficiency of the nerve pathway can be improved.

Complex integration of muscle and nerve activity
is needed to raise the arm over the head.

Development of efficient coordination gives improvement in the following areas:

- Quality of performance.

- Appropriate responses to balance control with rapidly changing body positions.

- Grace and beauty of movement.

- Protection against injuries attributable to awkward movement (coordination failure injuries).

- Efficiency of movement, decreasing chronic overloading of cartilage, bones and other connective tissue (stress injury).

POSTURAL STRENGTH AND COORDINATION

A good postural strengthening and coordination program in childhood is one of the most important areas to emphasize since it can lead to a healthier and injury-resistant adult.

Postural strength and coordination are usually the most neglected part of injury prevention. Even experienced athletes are injured because they have poor postural coordination, even though they are otherwise well-conditioned.

*Note the perfect posture that comes automatically in a young child. We are **born** with good posture. What happens?*

Postural coordination is a combination of agility, balance and timing that allows skillful execution of movement. This reduces the risk of injury and heightens the enjoyment of the sport. It is developed by using a great variety of sport-specific agility exercises and drills---also by specific postural coordination and strengthening exercises.

Growing bones will respond to stresses and extremes in poor posture. This can cause abnormal growth of bones due to the abnormal stresses. Most of us know that merely telling a child, "sit up straight," "don't slouch," or "pull your shoulders back" is not effective.

What *is* effective is to have good role models who demonstrate perfect posture. Talk to your children about the importance of good posture. Discuss how this can help them not only look better but become better athletes who are less likely to get hurt. Make postural exercises a regular form of exercise. If the parents understand this, the children will too. If the parents do these postural exercises, the children will do them as well.

Postural strength and coordination refer not just to spinal posture, but also to how the whole body is carried, including the arms and especially the legs. The muscular strength should be sufficient to hold the skeletal structure in good alignment during the shock and strain of exercise. If postural strength fails, the joints will move too far out of their normal range of motion (ROM), unduly stretching the tendinous or ligamentous structures, and injury will occur.

Postural strength should be developed with a series of supplemental exercises emphasizing the development of the muscles of the abdomen, waist, lower and mid back, buttocks, thighs, shoulder carriage and neck.

Muscle coordination is especially important in children. During this stage of growth, poor posture can lead to actual growth changes in the back and it certainly leads to more patterns of movement which in adult life can result in secondary back and hip problems.

We have all heard the saying, "You've got to tone up those muscles." But do we actually know what that means? Healthful muscle firmness is called "tone". A body out of shape, weak and unwilling to work, lacks the "tone" necessary to provide erectness of posture and the energy to accomplish the ordinary work requirements of daily life.

So you see, it is all interrelated. The skeletal system is supported by the muscle system and joints are held in place by ligaments that need to be strong. Muscles need to have strength, tone, endurance and flexibility and the nerve pathways need to function unimpaired so that they all work in harmony.

THE SKELETAL SYSTEM

The skeletal system is a framework held up by the muscle system. Together, they are called the musculoskeletal system, which is responsible for body movement. The skeleton serves three functions: it provides a rigid framework for the muscles to attach to, it helps protect the internal organs and it produces red and white blood cells in the bone marrow.

The musculoskeletal system upon which the body depends is composed of bones and their associated soft tissue. Ligaments, tendons, muscles, fascia, nerves and blood vessels: exercise can influence development of each of these especially in the growing athlete. It can be a very positive development, or if not done properly, can be a very disastrous development.

A *joint* is the site where two or more bones join together, whether or not there is movement between them. There are joints which do not move--- for example, the growth plates in children. However, we will discuss only two types of joints.

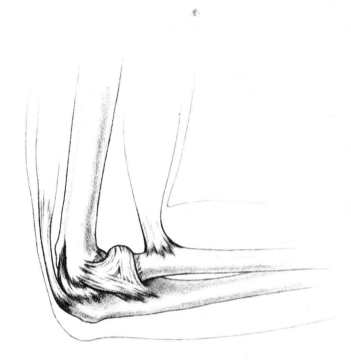

This illustration of the elbow joint shows the ligamentous structures laterally. The biceps muscle with its tendon attachment to the radius contracts, flexing the elbow. The triceps and triceps tendon attachment posteriorly contracts, extending the elbow.

The first type has little movement and is joined by a thick, fibrous tissue (or *fibrocartilage*). Examples are the discs between the bodies of the vertebra.

The other type of joints, the *synovial joints*, has the maximal amount of movement. Examples of these are the knee joints, finger joints, the elbow, the shoulder and the ankle joints. Most of our focus will be on the anatomy and function of synovial joints.

In the synovial joint, the bony surfaces are covered with a tough padding called *cartilage*. There is a sac surrounding each synovial joint called the *capsule*. A thin inner lining of the capsule, the *synovium*, secretes the lubricating fluid called *synovial fluid*.

SKELETAL GROWTH

From the time we are born until the time we reach full skeletal maturity (in the teenage years), the bones of the body are growing. During this time, they are composed of living cells, which are constantly dividing and multiplying and reshaping the bone. These small cells are surrounded by a material called the *matrix*. This matrix is incorporated with calcium to give the bone its hardness. The long bones of the body, those bones that for the extremities (the arms and legs), grow in length and width until skeletal maturity is reached.

Initially, our skeletal framework consists entirely of cartilage. This is converted to bone by a process called *ossification* (making of bone). After primary ossification, skeletal growth continues by continuously breaking down, reshaping and adding new bone. Some ossification takes place by first going through a cartilage growth phase and then converting the cartilage to bone. This takes place at the physis and epiphysis and is responsible for the growth in the length of long bones (arms and legs).

There is another form of ossification responsible for the growth in width of long bones and also the growth of flat bones (pelvis and skull). In this form, bone is created directly, without a cartilage phase.

There are many differences between bone and cartilage tissue. Bone tissue is harder and stronger and contains calcium. X-rays show the bone because of the calcium content.

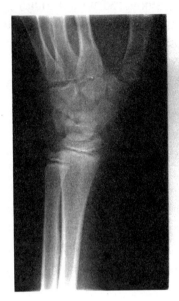 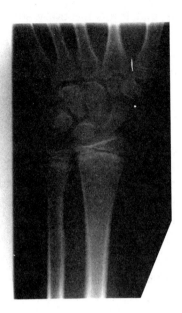

This x-ray of the long bone of a child shows the growth plate with epiphysis and the metaphysis.

The growth plate is the clear area seen between the two calcified bony areas. No calcium has yet been deposited on the growth plate, so it appears clear on the x-ray.

The word "*epiphysis*" comes from the Greek words, *physis*, which means *growth*, and *epi*, which means *upon*. The epiphysis is the cap-like portion above the growth plate. The *epiphysis* means "upon the growth plate." *Meta* in Greek means *after*.

Metaphysis means "after the growth plate." *Apo* means *offshoot*, and *apophysis* is a growth plate that appears as an offshoot from the bone.

Children are continuously influenced by their peers, mentors, and by their environment. The child out there for his/her first week of Little League practice, getting ready to pitch in a few pitches is not considering that his/her bones are growing and that repetitive motion may cause some damage to the natural growth of his/her elbow. In fact, limitation is hardly a part of the vocabulary of growing children. With proper supervision of athletic events and physical activities, overuse of athletic injuries in children can be avoided, leading to a healthier adulthood with fewer limitations.

One of the changes that occur to the muscles with exercises is *hypertrophy* or enlargement of the muscle fiber. As the muscle exercises, there is also an increasing number of capillaries that begin to nourish the muscle and the surrounding connective tissue. Thus the blood flow is improved when proper stress is applied, the connective tissues (fascia, tendons, ligaments and cartilage) will also *hypertrophy* (become thicker), (but at a slower rate than with the muscle tissue). The metabolism improves first. Then the muscles get stronger, while strengthening the connective tissue and bone takes longer to achieve.

The development of bone depends on the amount of load applied to the bone. In other words, bone develops stronger in areas that have more load applied. An inappropriate load or too much load, however, can damage the bone, as with stress fractures. Appropriate loads over a long period of time, on the other hand, cause an increase in bone strength along the lines of stress and lowers the likelihood of injury. We know that total inactivity of the bone results in bone absorption and weakness. This is true for ligaments, muscles and cartilage as well.

Cartilage is the articular covering on the ends of the bone, lubricated and nourished by the fluids secreted in the synovial membrane. Physical activity keeps the cartilage well nourished. Inactivity makes it soft and easily damaged. Inappropriate stress across the cartilage can damage it. Inappropriate stress across youthful cartilage can cause damage and growth disturbance. **The best method of keeping cartilage in good condition is gentle, appropriate exercise. Unbalanced, extreme loads should be avoided.**

Connective tissue connects and holds the body together. *Ligaments* and thick connective tissue surrounding the joint (*joint capsules*) work together to hold joints together. *Tendons* connect muscles to bones. *Fascia* is the "packing material" or webbing that surrounds, protects and holds muscles together. Ligaments, tendons, muscles and fascia are formed by connective collagen fibers.

Regular exercise preserves and increases the strength of the connective tissue, the joint capsule, the ligaments and the tendons. Inactivity, however, will cause decrease in strength. It is important in training to realize that the bone, ligament, and cartilage increase in strength at a slower rate than the muscles. **Just because your muscles are strong does not mean that other connective tissues are ready to handle a heavier load.** Muscles, with exercise, increase in size and strength. Inactivity affects muscles by decreasing their strength, their endurance, and their coordination, while increasing the risk of injury. Since the healthy, active muscle structure protects the joints and bones from injury by reducing the stress load imposed by impact, it is easy to understand the importance of keeping your muscles in good condition.

CHILDHOOD TRAINING AND CONDITIONING PROGRAM

The name of the game is to prevent injuries---proper training and conditioning can do just that. It is very important for children to learn the principles of training and conditioning. Hopefully, these principles will follow them throughout their lives as they pursue any athletic activities.

In general, the earlier the child gains certain specific skills, the better he or she will perform in sports. At a very early age, children can begin sports activities that require coordination, timing, agility and balance. These activities should be fun and emphasize coordination rather than strength or endurance. For instance, children can begin at pre-school age. These children can, with proper guidance, develop balance, agility, and coordination naturally.   Still, these activities should be approached carefully to make sure the child does not develop an injury or become fearful. Remember, pushing a child into an intensive program before the child is ready can be a detriment.

Proper training and conditioning in the young athlete is so very important. It can change his/her life forever, for better or for worse.

Each exercise activity should include:

- Warm up. This prepares the body for the forthcoming exercises.

- Conditioning. Here, the "sports specific" activities should increase gradually to better prepare the child's body for the sport.

- Cool down. Mild exercise, like walking or stretching after heavy exercise helps massage the waste products, i.e. lactic acids, out of the muscles. During this phase, the child adjusts to the decrease in physiological demands slowly rather than abruptly.

Pre-School Years - FUN, FUN, FUN!

During these years, the exercises the child experiences should basically be things that are **FUN**---carefully created games to play and, hopefully, parents to share them with. Since children are great imitators, they will pick up their attitudes and physical habits from their parents, coaches, and peers. During these younger years, a regular endurance or strength program is not necessary. Instead, it is important to emphasize, through example and fun things to do, good posture, balance, coordination and flexibility.

School Age - FUN AND FORM!

At this time, the child begins to enjoy more formal, more organized school experiences which should include organized and carefully monitored conditioning programs. Take care, though---this should not be very competitive. Instead, make it something **FUN**, reinforcing the importance of a regular exercise program and a positive attitude toward exercise and fitness. Include agility training, push-ups and sit-ups. **Form is more important than strength.**

Pre-Adolescent Years

During the years prior to puberty, training and conditioning programs can become more intense, more competitive, and last longer. It is important to remember, during this period of rapid growth, not to overstress the musculoskeletal system, causing growth plate injuries. Also, it is very important to emphasize flexibility and, again, a positive attitude. And remember, these are our children---winning is great---yes---but allow them to play for the love of the game.

Teenage Years

As young athletes begin to mature, they develop greater strength and muscle mass. Weight training in this age group may have benefits, **but still should not be overdone.** It is important, going into this phase, that the child have good posture, flexibility and coordination. Remember, the muscles will respond to exercise, by getting bigger and stronger. **The muscle patterns used in exercise and strength training will be strengthened.** Therefore, if teens are strengthening the wrong muscles, they can set themselves up for injuries down the road.

In other words, **it is important to strengthen muscles while using good form.** This is true for athletes of any age. The body works more efficiently from the proper position. If you have good form going into a strengthening phase, you will not only have fewer injuries, but you will be a better athlete.

It is very important for the parent and coach to understand some basic principles of the musculoskeletal system. In dealing with children, they are not miniaturized adults---children are different. The musculoskeletal system in children is still growing. It is important to understand the basic principles associated with that growth and anatomy in order to be able to identify and treat potential problems in children.

MUSCLE STRENGTH AND WEIGHT TRAINING

Muscle strength in children will definitely improve with strength training. This can happen naturally with a regular exercise program and athletics. It is important to carefully monitor any weight training prior to puberty. Weight training can be harmful due to joint overload on the ends of the long bones. If muscles are pulling too hard at the tendon bone attachment, they can pull off that vulnerable apophysis, causing abnormal growth in that area.

Training programs for growing children and children involved in athletics should involve specific training involving all muscle groups paying particular attention to the growing spine and proper positioning and form while using equipment. Any form of weight training should focus not on the actual amount of weight which the individual can bear, but should focus on frequent repetitions with well controlled movements avoiding excess stress of repetitive motions such as would be found in pitching.

Inappropriate strength training can cause actual damage to the joints themselves due to excessive weight placed across the growing cartilage and the growth plate at the joint level.

Joint abnormalities can occur and cause permanent damage to the joint. In severe cases, the growth plates can actually be shut down and no further growth can occur.

FLEXIBILITY - STRETCHING

> Flexibility and postural strengthening exercises should be as much a part of everyday activity as brushing your teeth.

Tight, rigid bodies are more susceptible to injury. Flexibility is important for injury prevention. Flexibility is also important in comfort and relaxation during heavy exercise, muscular speed and smooth, fluid movement. Conventionally, stretching exercises have been too heavily relied upon for warm-up prior to exercise. When used alone they do not provide an adequately thorough warm-up. They are important as a warming-up process, but are more important during the cool-down process.

> The phrase, "No pain, no gain," is dangerous when referring to exercises and stretching, especially in children.

Overstretching of the growing joints and muscles can lead to injury. Flexibility is best developed with a series of stretching exercises emphasizing the Achilles tendon, calf, back of the thigh, knee flexion, hip joint and spinal column. Faster and greater flexibility gains will be achieved when stretching is practiced **after** exercising. The development of flexibility requires daily practice of stretching exercises until flexibility goals are achieved. Again, it is important for children not to overstretch. Overstretching can cause injuries to the joints and actually end up with a laxity to the joints.

Pre-season physicals are a must. They should include flexibility tests so that if indeed certain flexibility problems are identified by the examining professional, programs can be instituted specifically for the individual child's needs. This can be set up through the school, the coach, or a sports medicine specialist. Certainly, proper stretching programs are very important.

Fitness in childhood is very profitable and positive. We know that physically fit children will, in general, do better in sports activities. When a child is involved in a proper fitness program first, there is a decrease in the injury rate. **The child will enjoy sports more and get hurt less.**

BASIC CAUSES OF SPORTS INJURIES

> Prevention of injuries in children is extremely important, because the consequences could lead to a permanent injury.

> **in-jure** *(in'jer) v.t.* **-jured 1.** to inflict bodily damage; to
> miss out on all the fun; to be hobbled; to spectate; to hang
> out with nothing to do; to be limping rather than playing;
> to not be able to take part in the game.

It is important to understand the three basic causes of sports injuries that
occur to the musculoskeletal system. These are injuries due to *direct
trauma, coordination failure* and *stress injuries*.

Direct trauma is an injury caused by hitting a person or an immoveable
object such as the ground or a tree or being hit by a baseball or a bat.
Direct trauma can cause fractures, joint dislocations, torn ligaments or
sprains. Also bruises or contusions can be caused by direct trauma.

Coordination failure, or a non-contact injury results from a momentary
loss of balance. This is a common cause of injury especially to the knee
or ankle. It can be a weight-bearing twisting injury and result in a torn
ligament, a sprain, a fracture or dislocation.

Stress injuries or overuse injuries can happen to almost any part of the
musculoskeletal system. It is a breakdown of tissues caused by repetitive
application of force at a rate exceeding the healing capacity of the tissues.
In short, a stress injury is a wearing-out process. This is especially
dangerous in children. This can cause breakdown of the growing tissue
and ultimately cause deformity of the joint or shortening of the muscle.
It can also cause fractures and growth deformities.

In baseball, unfortunately, there have been and still are many cases of
overuse injuries to the elbow and shoulder in the growing athlete due to
this process. That is why it is so very important to educate the parents
and coaches in the cause of the problem as well as to try to regulate the
amount of pitches thrown by the young athlete.

SOFT TISSUE INJURIES

Soft tissue injuries include contusions, hematoma, ligament sprains,
strains, bursitis, muscle cramps and soreness.

A <u>contusion</u> is commonly thought of as a bruise. This is usually caused by a direct blow to the soft tissue. The blow causes damage to the soft tissue resulting in bleeding into the damaged area. There is a clotting of the blood which stops the bleeding. The discoloration associated with this contusion is the accumulation of this clotted blood. The severity of the contusion depends upon the amount of damage caused by the direct blow. This is usually related to the location and the severity of the tissue damage.

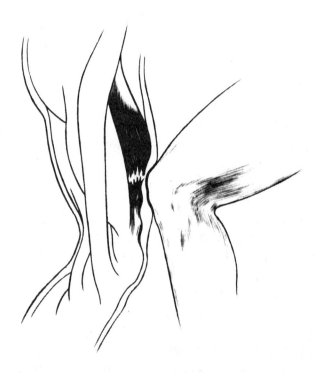

A contusion to the thigh muscles due to a direct blow.

More severe contusions lead to a <u>hematoma</u>, a more severe injury which causes a large accumulation of blood in the soft tissue. Accumulated blood clots in the soft tissue form a solid, swollen area. As it heals, the clot is slowly broken down and is absorbed into the body.

It is important to understand that hematoma is not a kind of clot that travels to the heart or the lungs such as a blood vessel. Hematomas are well localized and do not travel, but they can cause secondary problems, especially in children. This can lead to what is known as <u>myositis</u> <u>ossificans</u>, which is a secondary problem with hematoma. Instead of being completely absorbed by the body, the clot within the muscle will calcify (become hard with deposits of calcium). This condition needs to be seen and treated by a medical specialist.

Sometimes even a mild hematoma can cause a shutdown of a muscle and thus effect the joint. An example would be an injury to the quadriceps muscle which helps to stabilize the knee. With a weakened quadriceps, the knee is less likely to be stable and would be more vulnerable to injury.

LIGAMENTS

Joints are held in place by *ligaments*. Ligaments are strong, fibrous bands of collagen which have very little elasticity but are pliable. They reinforce the capsule and give stability to the joint. Ligaments attach from bone to bone between the two bone ends, giving static strength to the joint. In other words, the ligaments hold the joint together. If ligaments are torn or stretched, an unstable joint can result.

The thicker the ligaments are, the stronger they are and the better they support the joint from coming apart. A sprain happens when the joint is forced to move in an abnormal direction and the force exceeds the strength of the ligament. A *sprain* is a tear in the ligament, either a minor or a complete tear.

Most joints function much like a hinge to allow movement in the bony framework and, like a hinge, restrict movement to a given distance, or *range of motion* (ROM). Some joints function like a "ball-in-the-socket", and allow a greater ROM (shoulder, hip). The ROM of all joints is restricted by the capsule and ligaments. When a joint bends beyond its capacity (ROM), <u>immediate</u> damage results. For example, a strain/sprain injury can result in torn ligaments and muscle attachments, and/or ruptured synovial sacs. A damaged joint in a child can become the site of traumatic arthritis, and growth abnormalities.

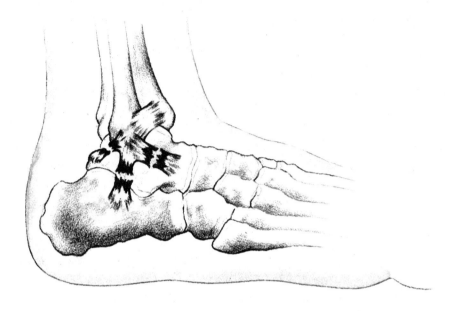

*Ankle Sprain. The ankle ligaments on the lateral aspect
of the ankle in this case are torn.*

Immediate treatment is the best method for dealing with
a contusion; *R*est, *I*ce, *C*ompression, and *E*levation,
commonly known as *R.I.C.E.*

R.I.C.E. results in less bleeding into the tissue, lessening the severity of
the injury. Certainly R.I.C.E. should be followed for the first forty-eight
to seventy-two hours. Massage should never be used at this stage. The
goal here is to restrict the motion, rest the affected area, and ice it. This
decreases the bleeding and swelling causing the blood vessels to constrict.

Use compression on the area such as wrapping with an Ace bandage. This also restricts further bleeding.   Elevation means keeping the limb higher than the heart, decreasing blood pressure in the area which also helps decrease bleeding.

LIGAMENT SPRAINS

A sprain is a tear of a ligament.   This can either be a partial tear or a complete tear.   Sprains are graded in degrees according to severity, first-degree being minimal, second-degree moderate, and third-degree severe. Tears of the ligament are usually due to *distraction* (pulling apart) injuries.   Forcibly exceeding the normal range of motion of a joint will tear the ligament, resulting in a sprain.

Complete dislocations of any joint results in third-degree sprains of the ligaments and capsules surrounding the joint.   It is important not to get this confused with the word *strain* - the only difference being that when the word "sprain" is mentioned, it is a ligament injury and when "strain" is mentioned, it refers to a muscle or tendon tear or injury.

Muscle is connected to bone by a tendonous structure and has an origin and an insertion.   The nerve enters the muscle and the impulse in the nerve causes the muscle to contract.   Without nerve impulses, muscles would not contract.   Skeletal muscles have thousands of narrow muscle cells.   These are contracting elements.   The muscle fibers work by shortening and lengthening.   Muscle attaches to tendons as it nears the bone and the tendon then attaches to the bone.   The junction where the muscle forms into the tendon is called the *musculotendinous junction*.   The mid portion of the muscle, the bulky part, is called the *muscle belly*.

The *fascia* is a strong fibrous tissue which gives support and holds together soft tissue such as muscles, tendons, nerves, and blood vessels. It is like a webbing throughout the body, surrounding it, holding as well as forming a shock absorption layer.   Each muscle is surrounded by these tough, fibrous fascia called *muscle sheaths*.

When you understand this basic anatomy, it is easier to understand muscles strains or the tearing of the muscle fibers.   It can be a complete muscle rupture or a minor strain where only a few fibers are torn. When fibers are torn, bleeding occurs which results in the hematoma. Immediate treatment is the same as for contusions, R.I.C.E.

> As many as a third of all sports injuries are attributed to muscle injury. They tend to heal in about three weeks, especially if R.I.C.E. is applied immediately.

In the growing athlete, repetitive muscle injuries can lead to chronic scar tissue and abnormal development of the muscle. When an injury occurs caused by a forceful pull of the muscle, sometimes instead of the muscle or tendon attached to it rupturing, the tendon pulls away taking a piece of bone. This is called an *avulsion fracture*. This occurs more frequently in children than in adults, since many times the bony attachment is still growing and is weaker than the musculotendinous junction. Therefore the piece pulls off. This can lead also to growth disturbances at the muscle attachment. This should definitely be avoided.

TENDONITIS

The body's response to tissue injury is inflammation. The tissue injury can be caused by overload or repeated microscopic injury to the musculoskeletal system. It can also be caused by pressure or friction and external trauma. Inflammation can even be caused by infection.

Acute inflammation is when there is one injury and the body responds to that injury. When this occurs, there will be increased blood flow through the area, warmth, pain and decrease in function. This inflammatory response can be decreased if acted upon quickly. The sooner the acute injury is treated by icing, decreasing the bleeding in the area, and limiting the amount of further injury, the more the inflammatory response will be decreased. The sooner it is treated, the sooner the injury will heal, and less scar tissue will be formed.

When the suffix "itis" is seen at the end of a word, it means *inflammation*. The first part of the word will tell the location of the inflammation. For example, *bursitis* is the inflammation the bursa; *tendonitis*, is the inflammation of the tendon; *arthros*, taken from the Greek reference to a *joint* (arthron), so *arthritis* means the inflammation of a joint, just as apophysitis is the inflammation around the apophysis, (the growth area at the tendon attachment) in a child.

Tendonitis is the inflammation of the tendon, or frequently, inflammation around the tendon. Often, inflammation of the tendon or tendon sheath is caused by repetitive micro-tears of the tendon due to the overload or overuse of the tendon.

Treatment for this kind of condition involves treating the cause of the overload and tearing of the tendon. Find out what the child is doing that is causing the injury as well as treating the inflammation itself. Certainly, R.I.C.E. is indicated when symptoms of tendonitis occur.

Tendon tears can vary in degrees in much the same way as muscle tears. There are first-degree, second-degree, and third-degree tendon tears. Frequently, a first degree tear can be called *tendonitis*. A small tear of the tendon can be healed by inflammation and scar tissue the same as a muscle tear. Many small tears, such as the type that happen within the rotator cuff (tendonitis)---seen in the shoulder---can develop into a complete tear or rupture.

Frequently in children the tendon attachment becomes sore and may be called *tendonitis* or apophisitis (if the the tendon inserts into an apophisis.) This can lead to growth deformities if ignored and untreated.

Another factor which contributes to tendon injuries is when the muscle has built up strength faster than the tendon. In other words, the muscle strength is out of proportion to the tendon strength or to the tendon attachment strength. This can contribute to both complete tears of the tendon or complete avulsion of the tendon. This also contributes to small tears in the tendon resulting in inflammation and tendonitis.

Since the muscle strengthens faster than the tendon, it is common to see this type of injury when the muscle actually pulls off the tendon attachment. This needs to be repaired surgically. **This is especially a problem in the adolescent athlete.**

SKELETAL INJURIES OR INJURIES TO THE BONE

Injuries to the bone may result in breaks that are called *fractures*. When we hear the word *fracture*, we think it means only a slight crack. That is not so. A fracture is a break in a bone, and it is serious. There are degrees of severity in fractures and these can be determined by x-ray. Fractures may be oblique, spiral, comminuted, or transfers. Whether the fractures are in the diaphysis of the bone or are epiphyseal- type fractures, it is very important that the fracture be treated properly in children, because they enter the growth plate. This can result in severe joint deformities if not treated properly. All fractures and dislocations in children should be seen by a specialist as soon as possible.

Fractures in children are different from fractures in adults, because the bone is still growing, and these injuries need immediate and special attention.

When a fracture pierces the skin, it is called a *compound* or *open fracture*. This almost always requires surgery to repair and prevent bone infection.

An *avulsion fracture* is when a tendon pulls loose with a piece of bone. This happens most frequently in adolescents, since their muscles and ligaments are stronger at this time than the bone. We discussed this condition earlier; however, it is important enough to be repeated. The important thing to know about fractures is that the soft tissue around the fracture, the muscle, bone, tendons, etc. are also injured when the bone is broken.

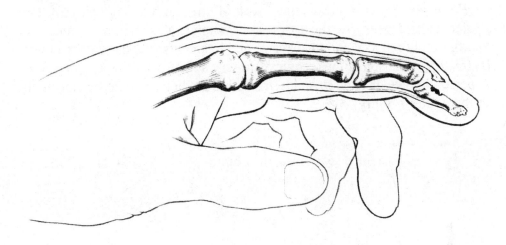

*Mallet finger deformity. A small avulsion of the
attachment of the extensor tendon. Without this
attachment, the finger will no longer extend.*

Broken bones must always be seen by a physician for appropriate
evaluation and treatment. The bone may need to be properly set so that
it, as well as the surrounding tissue, can be allowed to heal properly. We
call this reducing the fracture, or *fracture reduction*. The fractured bone
also needs to be held in place, or *immobilized*. This can be done by a cast
treatment or by surgical fixation of the bone - called *internal fixation*.

Sometimes a fracture cannot be put back in place properly without
surgery. This simply means that the bone had to be surgically put
together using either screws, wires, or rods, etc., which are designed
especially for this purpose. They are made from specialized stainless steel
metals. This is called *open reduction-internal fixation*.

A *dislocation* means that the two articular surfaces of a joint, previously in contact with each other, have been completely separated and no longer have contact.   This means that part of the capsule and part of the ligaments are torn.   In the case of a complete dislocation, it must be appropriately reduced and the capsule and ligaments which were torn must be treated. This sometimes requires surgery and a rehabilitation program. A person knowledgeable in children's sports medicine should be consulted in this type of injury.

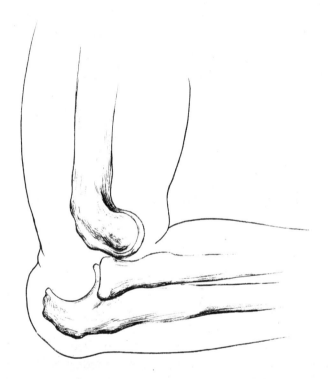

A complete dislocation of the elbow joint.

Stress injuries follow certain biomechanical principles. It is a simple rule. Tissue, whether soft tissue - tendons, ligaments, muscles, cartilage, etc.--- or bone, will break down when a force is imposed on it that exceeds its limit of strength.   Strength, of course, varies according to the type of tissue and its density, also according to the age of the person.

For instance, in an adult a stress injury might result in a stress fracture. In a child this might result in a breakdown of the cartilage and a breakdown of the growth plate, and would be much more severe.

Whether the tissue breaks or not depends on the type of force applied. A direct trauma, one major force, or many smaller forces that exceed the strength of the tissue, can cause it to break down. We compare the body to a coat hanger. The coat hanger will hold up a coat just as our musculoskeletal system will hold us up. If you try to tow a car with a coat hanger, it will break. If you hit it with an axe, it will be cut in two with just one blow. That would be an example of one force causing the breakdown of the material (direct trauma). Similarly, if we were hit by a car, tissues would break, (direct trauma).

Now apply the same reasoning, using many small loads to break the coat hanger. We know that if we bend the coat hanger repeatedly, it will eventually break. Repeated small traumas which exceed the strength of the area over a long period of time cause a breakdown of the tissue. Just like the coat hanger, the bone weakens and breaks apart.

Whole fields of study are developed to the treatment of fractures, and volumes of books have been written on this subject. Volumes of books have been written on children's fractures and children's orthopedics is a very specialized field.

GROWTH PLATES

In a child's bones, growth occurs from a remarkable structure, called a *growth plate*. As long as the growth plate is active, bone growth will continue. An active growth plate marks the difference between childhood and adulthood, as far as skeletal injuries are concerned.

The apophysis growth area is where a muscle-tendon attaches to bone. Prior to full growth, this is frequently an area of injury. When the forces across a muscle-tendon unit are too strong, the apophysis can be pulled away from bone, as in Osgood-Schlatter's disease.

Generally, active growth plates are usually weaker than the ligaments prior to the closure of the growth plates, so it is important to evaluate the growth areas of the bone when an injury near the joint is suspected. **Over half of the fractures occurring in the pre-teen years involve a growth plate.** Once the growth plates are closed, injury to a joint is more likely to be a ligament injury or a sprain.

> When bones, tendons, ligaments and cartilage are growing, injuries can occur which can effect young people, causing a permanent deformity such as injury to the growth plate.

The growth plate is not easily injured in the normal running and jumping stresses of childhood. However, excessive stresses across the growth plate, or breaks in the growth plate, can cause it to stop growing altogether or to grow in an abnormal manner, causing a deformity. Surrounding the growing bone is cartilage, also immature and vulnerable to excessive stresses which can cause cartilage damage and deformity.

Growth plates can be involved in problems other than direct injuries to the joint or stress injuries. There are diseases associated with the epiphysis in which it loses its blood supply. These problems require specialized treatment by an orthopedic surgeon.

Any time a child is experiencing pain in a joint, he or she should be evaluated by a physician. Any time a child is limping, that child should be carefully observed.

> If young athletes complain of pain, they should be listened to and evaluated.

Most of the growth plate injuries will heal without complications if protected and no further injury occurs. But it is important to have an orthopedic surgeon who is familiar with these types of injuries evaluate the child.

OSGOOD-SCHLATTER'S DISEASE

Many people have heard of Osgood-Schlatter's disease, a condition involving the growing attachment of the patellar tendon to the tibia (an *apophysis*). The exact causes are unclear. It seems to be a traction-stress type of injury, occurring in adolescence, in which a growing bone is pulled loose, causing inflammation. This will heal but may require casting. It seldom requires surgery. Physical therapy is important to regain the muscle coordination and strength after the inflammation has settled down.

LITTLE LEAGUE ELBOW

"Little League" elbow, unfortunately a common throwing injury, effects 12-20% of young pitchers. It is a serious injury that can easily be prevented. This injury may easily develop from a heavy pitching schedule. Although a Little Leaguer, by rule, can only pitch up to six innings per week, this only limits the number of innings he makes in competition as a pitcher. It does not limit the amount of hard throws he may pitch in practice, nor does the rule prohibit the same pitcher throwing the ball as a part-time catcher. **This is important to monitor.**

Studies have shown that injuries to the elbow in young athletes 9 to 14 years old are directly proportional to the number of throws executed.

Another factor in the injury rate of these young athletes is whether or not the child throws curve balls. If so, it is important to remember that the child stands a much higher risk of developing an injury.

During the acceleration phase, the thrower's arm pulls forward with the forearm lagging, putting much stress across the elbow. Problems in the medial side of the elbow are caused by pulling forces (distraction forces) called *valgus stress*. X-rays of the elbow may show changes in the growing cartilage and bone (the medial growth plate) of the young athlete.

The more severe problems, however, are on the lateral side, where repeated jamming or compression of the cartilage surface of the radius bone (radial head) against the *capitulum* (the upper portion of the elbow joint) may cause loss of blood to the radial head. When this occurs, loose pieces of cartilage and bone are often left in the joint, leading to arthritis.

About eight percent of younger pitchers had elbow x-ray changes showing some damage to the lateral side of the elbow. It is not uncommon to see loose pieces of cartilage, called loose bodies, in the elbows of teenagers who were pitchers at a younger age. Surgery is often necessary to remove the loose pieces in the elbow if the symptoms are pain, "locking" of the elbow and lack of full motion. Sometimes this can be done arthroscopically.

Understanding how the young body works, and how it becomes injured is important to prevention of injuries. Good throwing mechanics and pre-game warm-up, combined with good shoulder coordination and not throwing with "all arm" would help prevent many elbow problems in young athletes.

REDUCING INJURIES

Education in injury prevention for Little League coaches, parents and players should reduce injury rates. Proper certification before coaching or training young players is one proposed approach. Certainly a teamwork of education and communication between coaches, trainers, parents and players, through whatever effective means available, is definitely needed to reduce injury rates.

Young players should be educated and encouraged to report any type of soreness that may arise. There should be icing of the elbow following practice and play and decreased amounts of throwing altogether (such as missing rotations, not throwing in practice or not moving from pitcher to catcher's positions). All of this would help spare the arm of the Little League pitcher.

We have discussed injuries to the musculoskeletal system. These are the most common injuries and the most commonly neglected, but not necessarily the most severe. Certainly, head injuries can be the least obvious and potentially the most serious. When any head or neck injury occurs in a child, that child should be evaluated by a qualified medical professional.

> If symptoms of injury persist with the young athlete, x-rays should be taken and the Little Leaguer checked by a specialist. Abnormal stress put on growing and immature tissues can cause lifelong problems.

NUTRITION

Proper nutrition is important throughout the growing years, regardless of the participation in sporting events. The present push for health foods and active life-styles has greatly advanced public awareness for the need of nutritional and balanced meals. Many schools advocate healthy eating programs and supply children with well balanced nutritional meals.

The growing body has higher caloric needs and also is more susceptible to deficiencies in the diet. This is particularly true of children raised on vegetarian diets. Special care must be made to insure that these children receive enough of the essential amino acids and proteins required for proper bone and muscular growth.

The American diet is notoriously high in salt and saturated fats which are especially high in processed foods. Foods such as potato chips, peanut butter, iced cakes, cookies and candy bars are high in saturated fats and salts.

Healthy snacking provides an important supplement for the regular three meals per day diet. Parents need to supply the higher caloric needs of a growing and active individual. Avoid empty calories by providing snacks high in fibers and grains and low in fats, such as fresh and dried fruits, fresh vegetable sticks, low fat cheeses and yogurts, low fat, low sugar cookies and muffins. Low salt pretzels are an excellent munchy dry snack, high in complex carbohydrates and low in salt and fats.

Always check the nutritional information when buying processed snacks. Your child's caloric needs increase when participating in athletic events and diets should reflect the amount of energy expended.

High complex carbohydrates provide an easily digestible and quickly available form of energy. Pre-game meals should be high in complex carbohydrates and should be ingested from two to four hours prior to the event to take place. Fats should be avoided as they will not be available for immediate energy requirements. Fluid intake should be stressed prior to, during and after sporting events.

There are many electrolyte fluid supplements provided in local grocery stores. Athletes will find these especially useful during hot weather. Fluid supplements should not be used as dietary substitutes. Athletes require regular, balanced meals with adequate fluid intake (water, etc.) during the day to provide the calories necessary for proper growth.

STEROIDS

```
Saying YES to SPORTS
          is
Saying NO to DRUGS!
```

Steroids are out there and most athletes will eventually be faced with the question, 'Should I use them?'. Steroids are a natural chemical located in our bodies and are responsible for the natural progression of growth and development of all of our body systems. Unless we have an actual medical illness, our body knows exactly how many steroids we need, when we need them and where we need them. And this is a definite case where we should not be messing with Mother Nature.

Steroid abuse, or as some may like to believe, just plain old steroid use can and will have a direct affect on the ability of the growing body to mature naturally. Unfortunately, these drugs carry **serious** side effects, many of which are not measurable until severe damage has been done.

Steroids will cause atrophy or shrinking of the sexual organs and may lead to sterility. They have been implicated in liver disease, and the destruction of heart muscle. They are also responsible for acne, changes in sleep patterns, deepening of the voice, balding, increased aggressiveness and **premature closure of growth plates** in the long bones of children. The side affects are most severe in women and adolescents. **Many of these side affects are irreversible. These drugs are illegal, unethical, dangerous, and should be avoided.**

YOU AS THE CARING ADULT

We have discussed how the child's body works, how it can get injured, some ways of preventing these injuries and what to do if an injury should occur. We have known it is vitally important to understand the changing physiology during the child's growing years.

Youths in athletics or fitness programs cannot be dealt with as small adults. Their muscular and skeletal systems are constantly changing and developing, and unlike the adult body, they are open to injuries which could be detrimental to their growth and their future health. Also, since a primary cause of injury in children in sports is due to accidents related to poor equipment and lack of proper supervision, we can obviously make a difference in these injury rates through better understanding, education and adequate supervision.

Again, the coach, trainer and parents, must be aware of the wide range of strengths and abilities in any given age group during the growing years. They must be willing to adapt the sports program to the specific child's needs according to physical capabilities, growth and maturation.

The importance of physical fitness at any age cannot be over stressed. During the growing years, athletics should be fun, as well as safe. The young athlete should be provided with support, love and understanding from coaches and parents.

Providing a positive learning environment with realistic goals will allow a healthy understanding of competition, a raised sense of self-esteem, and will provide the basis for a future in athletics and fitness as an adult.

When working with youngsters, try to remember something essential about children. Children's bodies---and psyches---while they might appear on the outside to be very adult-like in nature, are in reality very fragile...They need extra support, extra understanding and extra love to make it all work.

XIII
Prevention of Common
Baseball Injuries

*"Injuries don't occur by chance,
they are often well coached."*

--Dr. Barton Buxton, A.T.C.

Introduction

In examining the factors that influence injury in sports, it is important to maintain a global perspective. This means that the all aspects of the sports should be evaluated for risk factors that can lead to injury. In the sport of baseball these factors are relatively specific and should be addressed in a logical sequence to decrease the threat of injury during participation. However, baseball is a contact sport, that involves high velocity, ballistic movements and player collisions. Therefore, the entire scope of traumatic injuries can occur during participation. The following chapter will focus on specific techniques of injury prevention, acute care, and common baseball injuries.

Prevention

Pre-Participation Physical Examination

The fact that children begin playing baseball at such a young age increases the importance of injury prevention. The musculoskeletal and physiological characteristics of a young athlete are drastically different from those of their older counterparts. These differences are directly related to growth and maturational status. Before participation, all athletes should undergo a complete physical examination. The pre-participation physical examination (PPE) is one of the cornerstones for injury prevention. A thorough PPE, performed by a physician, is essential in detecting pre-existing conditions and/or anatomical anomalies that may predispose an athlete to injury. The PPE should consist of a general physical examination with an extensive musculoskeletal and cardiovascular stress component. Further, the PPE should include a maturational assessment to determine the existing level of maturity in the athlete. Children, before adolescents, have active growth plates located at the ends of their long bones called epiphysis. These soft areas generate the foundation and out growth for the calcified structure of the bones in the elbow, wrist, shoulder, hip, knee and ankle. Overuse, overload or excessive stress can cause permanent damage to the growth plates. This damage can result in premature closure of the epiphysis and retard growth plates. This damage can result in premature closure of the epiphysis and retard growth in the long bones of the body. Growth plates' injuries in baseball were discussed in the previous chapter.

Medical History and Consent

Following the PPE it is sound practice to have a medical history form on all participating players. These forms should include information on existing medical conditions that may arise during participation, such as exercise induced asthma, to vital emergency information including drug allergies and medication currently being taken. These forms should be collected before participation by the coach and keep with them always during practice and competition. The forms have two purposes; first, to alert the coach of any pre-existing conditions that may limit the athlete's ability to participate. Second, in the instance of injury the form allows emergency medical personnel to have all the pertinent medical history information to expedite treatment. The medical history form should include a complete medical history, emergency contact information, insurance information, and parental consent for medical treatment.

Proper Conditioning and Training

Conditioning is an essential component to any sport and is a major factor in decreasing incident of injury. Baseball is primarily an anaerobic-ballistic action sport. Therefore, it is important that the conditioning program imitate the actions of the sport. This is called specificity training. Specificity training, like all training should be increased in a slow progressive fashion. The human body is designed to acclimate specifically and accommodate to change. These change results in adaptations in physiological function and response and allow the body to accomplish the imposed task more efficiently. However, if the load or resistance is too rapid or great, the body can not accommodate for it and will respond through injury. Therefore, it is essential that conditioning be done, but always progress slowly so that the athlete can accommodate the rate of change.

Although conditioning should be specific to baseball, conditioning should not impede with the teaching or patterning of technique. All fine motor movements in sports are patterned. Therefore, it is important that athletes develop motor skill when they are not fatigued. A concern in baseball is when athletes are asked to take batting practice at the end of a practice or following a conditioning session. Furthermore, conditioning should not be done at the beginning of practice. It will only fatigue athletes and decrease the ability to learn, and develop skills in sport.

Warm-Up and Cool-Down

The ability to prepare the body for activity is important in the prevention of injury. The body performs optimally when it is properly prepared for activity. The preparation should include a slow steady increase in heart rate and respiratory function. The specific patterning movements of the desired activity should also be introduced during the warm-up phase. In baseball, players should begin practice with a slow jog to increase metabolic activity. How warm is warm enough? The athletes should begin to break a sweat. This indicates that the athletes have increased their internal temperature enough for the body to begin to dissipate the heat generated. At this point specific activity to baseball should be introduced. Throwing activities should be started during the warm-up phase with a series of short toss activities, then long toss activities, followed by shoulder stretching. This allows the body temperature to increase and the resulting stretch is more effective. If the muscles in the shoulder have been exercised slowly they will respond to the impeding stretching. Other specific stretching can follow. The other areas of the body specific to the activity of baseball, are the legs, low back and upper torso. The pre-practice stretching should be limited to the activities that will prepare the body for practice. The majority of stretching should take place during the post-practice cool-down session.

During the cool-down period, athletes should "wind-down." This means that athletes should progress down following practice, just opposite to the increased progression that took place from the beginning of practice. The most effective stretching is done following practice. At this time the body temperature is still increased and the muscle will respond to the stretching process. During the cool-down phase the entire body should be stretched and players that have flexibility problems, that may increase incident of injury.

Proper Technique

The patterning of proper technique is essential in injury prevention. The majority of all shoulder injuries in baseball occur because of poor throwing technique. Throwing is a complex and integrated motor function that involves the entire body. The force that is generated during the throwing motion can cause extreme stress to the shoulder tissues. Slight changes in the biomechanics can disrupt the fine balance of maximum stress and tissue tolerance. It is essential that a coach be able to evaluate the throwing technique in order to prevent damaging shoulder and elbow injuries caused by poor mechanics in throwing. Pain during the different phases of the throwing motion can indicate an existing or potential shoulder injury. Shoulder and elbow injuries will be discussed later in this chapter.

Proper Equipment

Proper equipment plays an important role in injury prevention in all sports. It is a coach's responsibility to assure that the equipment be properly fitted and maintained. In baseball, all the equipment is essential for injury prevention. The proper outfitting of equipment begins with what the players wear. All baseball player's should be outfitted with supportive under garment and protective cup. The supportive cup can help prevent testicle injury during play. Next, all players should wear a pair of shorts that extend down the thigh. These shorts can help prevent injury when players slide. The outer garments in baseball should include the normal baseball pants and socks. The socks should always be worn into the pants to decrease the chance of skin exposure during sliding. Depending on the temperature and humidity, the layers and style of the shirt(s) worn in baseball can differ. If you are playing in hot, humid weather, it is important to have more area of the skin exposed on the upper body. This helps the body to dissipate the heat during exercise and keep cool. During cooler weather, it is wise to wear a long sleeve under shirt, with the uniform shirt on top. Finally, it is important all the equipment be cleaned frequently. Skin irritations can lead to bacterial and fungal lesions that may hamper or limit participation and in some cases be contagious.

The protective equipment in baseball should be fitted properly. All batting helmets should be fitted snugly on the player's head. The helmet should not move when the player turns his head from side to side or up and down. All batting helmets should have extended covers over the ears.

I recommend that all baseball helmets be fitted with a clear, polycarbonate face shield. This shield protects the face and the eyes from injury during baseball play. Eye injuries and facial fractures are common place and can be easily prevented. A final note concerning helmets: they should be worn always when players are batting and running the bases. This includes practice and cage work.

The one player on the field that is required to wear the largest amount of protective equipment is the catcher. The catcher's equipment is standard to the game. However, it is the coach's responsibility to assure that the equipment is properly fitted. The catcher's helmet should be snugly fitted on his head. It should not move when his head moves. The catchers mask should cover his entire face and there should be a comfortable cushion between his face and the mask. The mask should have a piece that extends down in the front to protect the catcher's throat. The piece should be made of a hard plastic. The catcher's chest protector should have adequate padding and cover the entire upper torso. The chest protector should extend downward to cover the entire groin area and genitalia. The catcher should always wear a protective cup. The cup will cover the genitals and should decrease the chances of testicular injury from a stray ball or collision. The catcher should wear leg guards that protect the knees, shins, ankles and the top of the feet. These guards should fit properly and be secured by elastic straps behind the legs. When the catcher assumes his position behind the plate, his front should be 100% covered with protective equipment. He should be able to move freely in his equipment and it should be worn always during practice and games.

Acute Care and Emergency Management

The proper management and acute care of baseball injuries should be of paramount concern to any coach. Any traumatic injury can lead to death. Injuries in the sport of baseball are no exception. If a young player was to get hit in the chest with a baseball, the force of impact could disrupt the normal rhythm of his heart and cause a heart attack. If a player was to get hit in the face with a line drive, the force of impact could cause a closed head injury, not to mention facial fractures and bleeding. If a player is rounding first base for what appears to be an easy double, and the left fielder one hops the ball on a dead run and guns it into second base, when the aggressive base runner slides and hits second base and the shortstop's foot at the same time, the force of the collision could cause a compound, dislocated fracture of the base runner's ankle. These are three injury scenarios that are not unlikely to occur during the course for a baseball season. Unfortunately, the coach is often the "first responder" in any injury scenario. Therefore, it is important that the coach be prepared to handle the situation, adequately treat the player's injury, and elicit emergency support when needed.

Emergency Management Plan

The emergency management plan (EMP) is a written document that describes what action should be taken if an emergency occurs during baseball practice or a game. The EMP should be a step by step plan of action that details who performs what duties and when during the emergency. The plan should include primary assessment of the situation; checking the player's level of consciousness, whether the player is breathing and whether the player has a pulse. If the answer to any of these questions is NO, emergency medical systems (EMS) should be notified immediately (in most areas this is done by calling 911). The EMP should account for who make the EMS call. The nearest phone should be indicated on the plan. If the person that is in charge of placing the call is absent a back-up should be incorporated into the plan. Once EMS has been activated the coach is then responsible for life support until the ambulance arrives.

If the player is conscious, breathing and has a pulse, a secondary assessment is needed to evaluate the situation. The problem may be apparent, such as the case above where the player has a fractured lower leg. However, there may be a number of injuries and the most evident one is not the worst. The secondary assessment should be completed quickly and thoroughly. Ask the player where they are experiencing pain. Pain is the body's way of alerting us to damage or the threat of damage. Once the player has pointed out the pain, examine the area for deformity and pain to the touch. Once the injury scenario has been assessed it is the coach's decision on whether or not to notify EMS for transport of the injured player. Common sense is always the best guide. If you believe that the injury is severe enough to warrant EMS, then activate them. The best rule of thumb is to always error on the conservative side.

The best way to complete an EMP is to practice using a mock emergency situation. Have a player lie down on the ground and feign an injury. Begin in a step by step manner and document what you did. Remember it is difficult to cover every scenario, so allow your plan to be generic enough to cover all situations. Once you have a plan you need to practice it. It does not take a long time to practice an EMP once a week to be sure that when an injury does occur that you are prepared.

Personal Training

In the event of an emergency situation it is imperative that the coach be prepared to handle any situation that arises. This preparation should include standard first aid and CPR. All coaches should be certified in first aid and CPR before the season begins. This will insure that you are prepared professionally in the event of any injury emergency. Injuries are apart of the game of baseball. If you are not prepared to handle the injury situation, then you are not totally qualified to coach! These courses can be taken at local high schools, colleges, and at the American Red Cross.

Pain

Pain is the body's way of alerting us that there is a threat to the normal function. In baseball, pain can be the most important key in discovering injury. Remember, athletes are not supposed to be in pain. If a player reports that he is in pain this is an important sign that something is wrong. Pay attention to these signs and listen to what the player is telling you. The anatomical location of pain and the movement that causes it are usually precise indicators of the problem. A functional evaluation can usually help discover the cause of the pain and lead to proper treatment of the problem. Always keep in mind that the pain is a symptom, not the problem. Therefore, once the pain is noticed the problem must be identified and fixed, or the pain will return and continue to plague the player.

Standard Injury Treatment

The standard first aid in almost all acute injury situation should include the following: **P**rotect, **R**est, **I**ce, **C**ompress, and **E**valuate (PRICE). To protect the injury means to splint or immobilize the injured area. This becomes especially important when a joint has been injured. Rest infers that once injury occurs activity should be stopped. Further activity will promote more injury and compound the existing problem. It is not wise to "run it off." The placement of ice on an injured area cools the area, decreasing the blood flow, metabolism and helps to relieve that pain by provided an anesthetic effect. The cooling of the injured area is important in decreasing the secondary effects of the swelling that accompanies trauma or injury. The ice should be applied as quick as possible. If the ice is applied within the first three minutes following injury the damage of the secondary swelling can be decreased dramatically. The effects of compression are also profound. The application of compression can reduce the amount of swelling associated with normal injury response. When used concomitantly with cooling, compression helps to decrease the initial response of the injury and decrease the healing time of the injury. Finally, elevation is used to decrease the amount of swelling that can accumulate in the injured area due to gravity. When these techniques are used in conjunction with each other they can influence the amount of recovery time following injury.

Recognition of Common Baseball Injuries

Most injuries are caused by the translation of generated forces to the human structure. In the evaluation of the injury that occur during baseball it is advantageous to examine the forces related to the sport. Most baseball injuries are relatively sports specific. The more common injuries occur in the shoulder and arm complex and are due to the forces generated during throwing. However, as with any contact sport, baseball injuries can occur to any portion of the body.

Shoulder

Because throwing is the primary movement in baseball, the shoulder complex is the most common area of injury in the sport. To understand shoulder injuries, one must first understand the structure and function of the shoulder complex. The shoulder is compromised of four joints: sternoclavicular, acromioclavicular, glenohumeral, and scapulothorasic. The glenohumeral joint is the major joint in the shoulder. The joint is composed of the head of the humerus and the shallow glenoid fossa on the scapula. The head of the humerus is three times larger than the glenoid fossa. Therefore, the structural stability of the joint is limited. The primary stabilizers of the glenohumeral joint are the glenoid labrum (a fibrocartilaginous ring that originates from the joint capsule), the joint capsule and the muscles of the rotator cuff (supraspinatus, infraspinatus, teres minor, and subscapularis). The glenoid labrum acts to increase the socket aspect of the glenoid fossa. The joint capsule provides some stability for the joint during external rotation due to increased ligamentous strands in the anterior capsule. However, the primary support for the joint is supplied by the rotator cuff muscles that blend into the capsule and help to stabilize the humeral head during shoulder motion. The structure of the shoulder and its musculotendinous support allow the shoulder extensive mobility. The shoulder has five basic ranges of movement: flexion, extension, abduction, adduction, (pure adduction is limited by the trunk) and axial rotation. The most important motions in baseball are abduction and rotation.

As previously mentioned (Chapter 6) the phases of throwing include: stance, wind-up, cocking, acceleration, and follow-through. During the wind-up phase of throwing the shoulder motion begins. The arm is extended back with slight external rotation. During the cocking phase, the shoulder becomes abducted in extension with marked external rotation. The cocking phase "loads" the force and prepares the muscles for the throw. In the acceleration phase the existing force is generated forward and the arm and shoulder begins to rotate internally. When the ball reaches the ear level it is released and the arm continues to move forward with the shoulder internally rotating. During follow-through the head of the humerus is distracted from the glenoid fossa. As the follow-through continues the triceps acts to decelerate the arm. The remaining force is then translated down through the arm. The final movement of the follow-through leaves the forearm in a pronated position with the thumb turned downward. Due to excessive force generated during the throwing motion the structures of the shoulder can become injured.

To properly recognize and evaluate a throwing related injury, the area of pain must be located. If the pain is generalized or in the upper front of the shoulder a rotator cuff lesion may be present. If the pain is radiating down the arm a nerve entrapment injury may be present. The second step in the recognition and evaluation of shoulder injuries in baseball relates to the type of pain that the player is feeling. A dull ache that may be more prominent at night is characteristic of a rotator cuff lesion or tear. Numbness is indicative of a nerve related injury. A burning type pain is more characteristic of a bursitis or tendonitis injury in the shoulder. It is important to find out if the player has any other related symptoms, such as a grinding, popping, or snapping feeling in the shoulder. The popping or snapping could indicate a labrum tear and the grinding is indicative of degenerative changes or chronic bursitis. Finally, the coach should evaluate the throwing motion. This is performed to identify the motions which cause pain or during which phase of throwing motion the player feels pain. If the player feels pain during the cocking phase or early acceleration phase of throwing, this may indicate one of the following problems: (1) deltoid strain, (2) bicipital tendonitis, (3) subluxation of the biceps tendon, or a (4) subdeltoid bursitis. If the player has pain from the acceleration phase to the follow-through, he may have one of the following problems: (1) rotator cuff impingement, (2) tendonitis of the pectoralis major, (3) tendonitis of the latissimus dorsi, or (4) tendonitis of the subscapularis. Finally, if the player reports pain during the follow-through, he may be experiencing one of the following problems: (1) anterior subluxation, (2) posterior subluxation, (3) posterior capsulitis, or (4) triceps tendonitis. Due to the translation of force during throwing, many injuries occur during the follow-through phase. It is essential that all throwing athletes perform a complete follow-through to allow the generated force to be dissipated through out the entire motion.

Once the throwing motion has been evaluated it is essential that the athlete be evaluated by a physician in order to make a final diagnosis. Physicians with expertise in the area of sports medicine are well trained in the area of sports related injuries. Therefore, it is helpful that the physician be told when the pain occurs precisely, since the physician is not usually present when the injury occurs.

If a young athlete reports shoulder pain while throwing, the coach should immediately refer the player to a physician for evaluation of a possible growth plate injury. As previously mentioned, the growth plates are soft areas of bony growth located at the ends of long bones. The repetitive stress, resulting from the throwing motion can cause growth plate damage to the shoulder. Small fragments of bone are pulled away from the musculotendinous insertions. This can result in premature closure of the growth plates, as well as permanent damage to the shoulder.

Other related shoulder problems can occur from repetitive throwing at high velocity. The arm was not designed to throw a 5 ounce object, at maximum velocity, repetitively. Therefore, the resulting stress causes overload to the tissues and the result is injury. Many times baseball players that throw too much will report pain on the tops of their shoulders. This subacromial pain is often associated with subacromial or subdeltoid bursal lesions. These lesions impair the throwing motion. This problem is usually associated with poor throwing mechanics. Often the player will throw with his elbow down and "short-arm" the ball.

Elbow

As with the shoulder, the elbow is an area that is susceptible to injury during throwing. The structure of the elbow is fairly unique. The two bones that make up the forearm, the ulna and the radius, cross over each other during forearm pronation. The concave head of the radius articulates with the rounded head of the capitulum and allows the radius to rotate during pronation. This motion is important in throwing. However, excessive, high velocity pronation can cause injury. Again, caution needs to be warranted with younger players that are susceptible to growth plate injuries in the elbow. Repetitive stress, from throwing can result in "little leaguers elbow." Little leaguers elbow results from excessive medial stress during throwing. The resulting stress can cause avulsion fractures on the medial epicondyle of the elbow. These lesions can cause permanent damage to the growth plate and produce bony lesions that impinge elbow movement. Restraint should be used in allowing the young pitcher to throw too often. Restraint should also be warranted in the use of curveballs and sliders with immature pitchers. The key to decreasing the incident of injury in the elbow revolves around the use of proper throwing technique, proper warm-up and cool down, and restraint from over-use.

Other related elbow injuries include a tear of the medial collateral ligament in the elbow and ulnar nerve entrapment. A medial collateral ligament tear occurs from traumatic overload. The player may have had pain in the medial aspect (inside) of his elbow for some period of time and suddenly felt a pop or tear during high velocity throwing. The player will demonstrate increased motion during valgus stress and pain over the common flexor tendon when making a fist. The player with ulnar nerve entrapment may report pain over the medial aspect of the elbow. This pain may occur as the result of falling on the elbow or following a throwing session. The primary symptom is numbness in the little finger and on the outside of the ring finger. All elbow pain and dysfunction should be evaluated by a physician as soon as possible. Caution should be exercised when placing ice over the medial aspect of the elbow, due to the location of the ulnar nerve.

Hand

Most hand injuries in baseball are related to the fingers. These finger injuries can be debilitating if not properly recognized and managed. The most frequent finger injury in baseball is the extensor mechanism injury. This injury occurs from a fracture at the distal end (tip) of the finger or a rupture of the extensor mechanism. The injury will result from direct force to the end of the involved finger. The result will be a "drop" finger or "mallet" deformity at the distal interphalangeal joint (DIP) (tip) of the finger. Initial treatment should include splinting the joint involved in extension and clinical evaluation. All finger injuries that entail possible fracture or dislocation should be evaluated by a physician, preferably a hand specialist.

Knee

Traumatic knee injuries in the sport of baseball are not common place. The numbers of ligamentous sprains and meniscal tears are dramatically lower in baseball than compared to other sports such as football, basketball, and soccer. Primarily the knee injuries in baseball involve growth related trauma, contusions and strains.

The most common growth related trauma to the knee is called Osgood-Schaltter's condition. This condition was previously discussed in chapter

XII, growth and development. Primarily, it is important to note that warm-up and stretching before and after participation can reduce the chances of rapid onset. However, during the acute stages of Osgood-Schaltter's condition, rest, ice, and compression will usually allow for adequate healing and decreased symptoms.

Contusions to the knee are relative common in baseball, especially at the catcher's position. It is important to stress that proper equipment and equipment fitting can reduce the incident and the severity of the contusion to the knee area. However, when a contusion does occur to the knee area proper management can further reduce the length of disability. Proper management should include rest, ice, compression, and elevation.

Concerning knee injuries in baseball, muscle strains are more common than ligamentous sprains because baseball does not require many cutting type motions. Muscular strain to the knee can include the muscles of the quadriceps group (front of the thigh) or the hamstring group (back of the thigh). Muscle strains will be reported following quick acceleration or deceleration movements. The player will report pain in the area of the strain, that increases with movement and stretching. Once a knee area strain has been reported, the athlete should be removed from participation and treated with ice, compression, and elevation. Follow-up referral depends on the extent of the injury. If the athlete has marked limitation such as the inability to walk, he should be evaluated by a physician. Further, if the strain is accompanied by marked discoloration the player should be evaluated by a physician.

Lower Leg

The lower leg and ankle complex are commonly injured in baseball. Traumatic ankle injuries are frequent and result from the player sliding into stationary bases and other players. The most common mechanism of ankle injury in baseball is related to the player "rolling his ankle over" and spraining the lateral ligament in the ankle. If the generated force is great enough, the resulting injury can include both an ankle sprain and a lower leg fracture. Ankle sprains can also occur due to players running in the field and turning their ankle in holes or over raised areas in the turf.

Once an acute ankle injury has occurred it is important to check for deformity and any immediate discoloration or swelling in the area. Marked deformity, swelling, and discoloration can all be indicative of a fracture or a bad sprain. If any of these three signs are present or in combination, the player's ankle and lower leg should be splinted and evaluated by a physician. If the ankle appears relatively normal following injury but the player is complaining about pain, a fracture should be ruled out. A simple percussion test can be done by the coach to aid in ruling out a fracture. The coach simply taps on the players heel with the palm of his hand. If the player reports pain higher up the ankle a referral should be made to a physician. Lastly, if the player reports pain, yet has comparable range of motion with the opposite ankle, and a negative percussion test, physician referral is not be an immediate concern. Ankle injury treatment should begin immediately. Ice and compression should be applied and the ankle should be elevated. Coaches are often concerned about whether they should remove the cleat and the sock to treat the injury. If the cleat and sock can be removed without causing further trauma it is advisable. The application of ice and compression should be initiated as soon as possible following injury. Once the ice and compression have been applied the ankle should be elevated above the heart to prevent the accumulation of swelling in the area.

Box Score

Prevention is the key.
Eliminate any possible problems before you begin.

✓ Technique
✓ Equipment
- Specificity in conditioning and training
- Add specificity to warm-up
- Majority of stretching in cool-down

Be prepared for injuries

Standard Care = P.R.I.C.E.

Listen to the pain
Look for the pain
Find the cause, don't just treat the symptoms.

XIV
Physical Conditioning

"We train movement, then muscle."

--Dr. Coop DeRenne

Physical conditioning is very important for the youth baseball player. Coach, if you take the time to emphasize physical conditioning to your team, then it will become a part of their athletic maturation.

Through the proper physical conditioning, fundamental-mechanical conditioning, and visual conditioning programs, your players will learn at a very early age the concept of holistic conditioning. They will understand that their athletic development can be enhanced and accelerated if all their bodily systems are conditioned properly through the holistic approach. Again, the holistic conditioning components are: (1) physical conditioning, (2) nutritional conditioning, (3) biomechanical conditioning, (4) visual conditioning, (5) mental conditioning, and (6) injury prevention.

Physical conditioning is a function of stamina, speed, strength and power. These physical conditioning components can be obtained by baseball players of all ages. You should understand that the above physiological fitness components will result through the proper weight training, anaerobic, and nutritional training programs. We want a fast and powerful lineup, not heavy, slow and weak bench jockeys.

The proper physical conditioning program will provide your players with at least the minimal strength, power, and anaerobic requirements that they need in order to compete successfully at their respective baseball level. Many times a young player gets "cut" in tryouts, or rides the bench as a non-starter not because he is less skilled, but because he is too physically weak. Coach, also your starting players may fall into slumps because of fatigue which is a sign that their conditioning base was too low. Watch for signs of fatigue.

Potentially, the well-conditioned player will be able to come closer to his optimized performance level more than the unconditioned athlete. He will have the extra "heater" in the late innings to blow away the powerful hitter, or the extra stamina to perform optimally in the late innings as well as over the long season. The highly conditioned athlete will also be able to withstand the demands of the game reducing the possibilities of seasonal and career threatening injuries.

All movement is dynamic in nature. In other words, when the player runs, throws and hits, he is moving over a prescribed distance in a certain amount of time. In order for the player to move more functionally, he must become more powerful. Why? All movement requires a certain level of strength and speed. The combination of strength and speed is POWER.

Baseball has a variety of dynamic movements. Baseball, therefore, is a strength and power-ballistic sport. It involves the velocities of a pitched ball, the swinging of a high speeding bat, and power for sprint-running. Strength and power are both weight training qualities that are essential to executing high speed ballistic throws, bat swings, running and stealing bases. To train the players for the demands of the game remember this principle:

> **Baseball is a ballistic sport over a marathon season.**

Specific Weight Training Program

Specificity: Power and Technique Training

MEDICINE BALL DRILL:
Swing Technique & Power

FOOTBALL:
Overload & Throwing Technique

4-OUNCE UNDERLOAD BASEBALL:
Technique & Arm Speed

Strength training for the prepubescent athlete (approximately 10-15 years old) has been an area of misunderstanding and misconception for many years. Many parents and coaches question the validity of even having a strength training program for this age group. Current research supports strength and power training for the prepubescent child. Therefore, strength training is essential to player's overall fitness needs.

The National Strength and Conditioning Association, (NSCA) has officially taken a medical and exercise stand that strength training for the prepubescent athlete is both "efficacious and safe when performed according to the NSCA guidelines."

The parent and coach who desire an ALTERNATIVE STRENGTH DEVELOPMENTAL PROGRAM for this adolescence age group should use a "PRESSING BODY WEIGHT PROGRAM." An athlete in this age group who is not physically mature enough to lift weights can acquire strength gains from working against his own body weight. This is accomplished by doing push-ups, pull-ups, dips, chin-ups and sit-ups. A full range of motion must be used with these exercises.

Dad and Mom, remember athletes mature at different rates. If you are going to use the alternate "body press resistant program," you may want to use the "shaving rule" as a guideline when to begin a weight training program for the athlete in question. If the athlete does not shave, then he does not need to lift weights.

The National Strength and Conditioning Association's Baseball Committee developed a physical and conditioning program for the prepubescent and post-pubescent baseball players. Tables 1 and 2 describe in precise detail this conditioning program. Dr. Coop DeRenne is a member of this elite baseball committee and we can highly recommend this conditioning program.

Anaerobic Training

There is a gross misconception in the game today that baseball is aerobic in nature. Traditionally, the majority of professional and amateur baseball programs have used aerobic training (long distance) to condition their players---running lap after lap and mile after mile.

Baseball is an anaerobic sport---short, quick and explosive movements in less than 15 seconds. All baseball plays occur within 15 seconds: hitters exploding out of the batter's box and sprinting around the bases, base stealing, base running, defensive players reacting quickly while fielding ground balls, line drives, and chasing down long fly balls in the gap, and pitchers ballistically throwing to a catcher.

The energy for baseball players to react in this ballistic game is the result of anaerobic metabolism. Anaerobic metabolism provides the short-term quick energy source to the cells. All baseball players must condition themselves anaerobically.

Baseball, as we have said, is a ballistic-power sport. Base runners and hitters need to condition their legs for exploding out of the batter's box, for bursting take-offs while base stealing, and for running around the bases. Pitchers also need to train anaerobically. Pitchers' legs are constantly in motion during their mechanical deliveries. As Hall of Famer Tom Seaver says as he puts sprinting into the proper perspective, "You are only as good as your legs."

Therefore, you must train your players anaerobically through interval training to meet their competitive game demands. An example of interval training follows:

- For the Base Runners and Hitters

    - Daily wind sprints of 30 and 60 yards during the off-season
    - Daily wind sprints of 8-10 yards and 30-60 yards during the season
    - 1st step lead-off base stealing sprints (5-7 reps) for reaction time

- For the Pitcher

    - Daily wind sprints of 30-60 yards during the season and off-season.

Coach, do not worry that your players are not getting enough fitness training. These anaerobic wind sprints will have enough aerobic carry-over value.

To prevent seasonal or career ending throwing injuries with your pitchers, adhere to the following in-season guidelines.

- Daily: Stretch, general warm-up, throwing warm-up sequence

- Range of motion resistance training with light dumbbell and stretch cord programs

- Daily: Anaerobic sprints

- GRADUALLY AND SYSTEMATICALLY increase the amount of game pitches under close supervision.

- ONE WEEK REST BETWEEN STARTS for your starting pitchers, and THREE DAYS rest for a reliever who threw 3 innings. NEVER throw your reliever two consecutive days.

In summary, strength, power and anaerobic training is essential for the serious prepubescent athlete. The program we recommend is found in Tables 1 and 2.

TABLE 1: Pre-Pubescent
Weight Training Program

WARM-UP

Exercise	Season	Duration/Vol.	Intensity	Rest
Easy Run	Year Round	3-5 min.	(L)	
Dynamic Flexibility a. Arm Swing b. Leg Swing c. Trunk Rotation		5 min. (max)	(M)	
Static Stretches:		total body 5 min.	(M)	

MOVEMENT SKILLS

Exercise	Season	Duration/Vol.	Intensity	Rest
Skipping Side Stepping Plant & Cut Sepintin Run Backward Run 360° High Skip Back Peddle Line Touch Jump Rope	Year Round	10 min. total		

THROWING CONDITIONING

Exercise	Season	Duration/Vol.	Intensity	Rest
Crow Hop Throw (Flat ground) (Flat shoe)	O,P,I	5 oz., 10 throws x 1 6 oz., 15 throws x 1 4 oz., 15 throws x 1 5 oz., 10 throws x 1	60'/90'/120'-200' 120'-200' 120'-200'	

Pre-pubescent
FUNCTIONAL STRENGTH:

Exercise	Season	Duration/Vol.	Intensity	Rest	Frequency
Core	Off-Season	3-5 sets, 4-12 reps	60-95% of	2-4 min.	3 days/wk
Supplemental		2-5 sets, 8-12 reps	10RM		(M-W-F)
Core	Pre-Season	3-6 sets, 2-8 reps	60-90% of	2-3 min.	3 days/wk
Supplemental		2-4 sets, 6-10 reps	10RM		
Core	In-Season	1-3 sets, 6-10 reps	60-85% of	1-2 min.	1-2 days/wk
Supplemental		1-2 sets, 8-12 reps	10RM		

Core Exercises include (in sequence):
*1. Bench Press
2. Lats Pull-down
3. Leg Curls
4. Leg Extensions
  Squats (post-pubescent)
5. Bicep Curls
6. Triceps

Supplemental Exercises include:
1. Wrist Curls
2. Dr. Frank Jobe's shoulder exercises (Continela Hospital, Inglewood, CA)
3. Heavy-Light-Standard bat swings (only in O,P seasons)

*In-Season = dumbbell press

SPEED:

Exercise	Season	Duration/Vol.	Intensity	Rest	Frequency
Accelerate	O,P,I	10-50 yds.	(H) 200-300 yds	Complete	Daily
Lateral jumps or steps	O,P,I	3-5 sets	(H) 8-10 reps	Complete	Daily

SPEED STRENGTH:

Exercise	Season	Duration/Vol.	Intensity	Rest	Frequency
Rope Jump	P	2-4 sets of 150-400 reps	(L) 17-100 contacts	1-2 min.	3 days/wk
In Place Jump	P	3-6 sets of 10-20 reps	60-120 contacts	1-2 min.	3 days/wk
Short Response/ Long Response	P	3-20 sets of 3-10 reps	40-200 contacts	2-3 min.	3 days/wk
Upper Body	P	4-10 sets of 10-20 reps	40-200 contacts	1-2 min.	3 days/wk
Plyometrics	P				3 days/wk

IMPLEMENTATION:
SPEED STRENGTH:

Exercise	Season	Duration/Vol.	Intensity	Rest	Frequency
Bat Swings	O	9 wks. 1 oz. every 3 weeks to 29 oz. (Max.)			Daily
	P	periodic 1 oz. drops to 25 oz.			
Dry Swings Batting Practice		Min. 50 cuts/bat	Stand.-Hvy.-Lt.-Stand. Max. 100.bat	50-100	Daily
T-Work					
	P	1 oz. below no more than 2 oz. above weight of in-season bat			
	I	normal weight bat as much as time permits			
Medicine Ball and			2-3 kg.		Daily
Stride Length Box Combination	O,P,I	3-5 sets x 10 reps		1-2 min.	Daily

SPEED ENDURANCE

Exercise	Season	Duration/Vol.	Intensity	Rest
Sprint	O,P,I	(50-300 yds) x 1-3, 1-5 reps	(90-100%)	:45-complete (reps) 3:00-complete (sets)

O = Off-Season L = Light
P = Pre-Season M = Moderate
I = In-Season

TABLE 2: Post-Pubescent Weight Training Program

WARM-UP

Exercise	Season	Duration/Vol.	Intensity	Rest	Frequency
Easy Run	O,P,I	3-5 min.	(L)		Daily
Dynamic Flexibility		5 min. (max)	(M)		Daily Daily
a. Arm Swing					
b. Leg Swing					
c. Trunk Rotation					

MOVEMENT SKILLS

Exercise	Season	Duration/Vol.	Intensity	Rest	Frequency
Skipping	O,P,I	10 min. total			Daily
Side Stepping					
Cara.					
Plant & Cut					
Sepintin Run					
Backward Run					
360°					
High Skip					
Back Peddle					
Line Touch					

THROWING CONDITIONING

Exercise	Season	Duration/Vol.	Intensity	Rest	Frequency
Crow Hop Throw	O,P,I	5 oz., 10 throws x 1	60'/90'/120'-250'		Daily
(Flat ground)		6 oz., 15 throws x 1	120'-250'		
(Flat shoe)		4 oz., 15 throws x 1	120'-250'		
		5 oz., 10 throws x 1			

Post-Pubescent Weight Training Program
Table 2, page 2

FUNCTIONAL STRENGTH:

Exercise	Season	Duration/Vol.	Intensity	Rest	Frequency
*Core *Supplemental	Off-Season	3-5 sets, 4-12 reps 2-5 sets, 8-12 reps	60-95% of 10RM	2-4 min.	3 days/wk (M-W-F)
Core Supplemental	Pre-Season	3-6 sets, 2-8 reps 2-4 sets, 6-10 reps	60-90% of 10RM	2-3 min.	3 days/wk
Core Supplemental	In-Season	1-3 sets, 6-10 reps 1-2 sets, 8-12 reps	60-85% of 10RM	1-2 min.	2 days/wk

*see Pre-Pubescent Table 1

SPEED:

Exercise	Season	Duration/Vol.	Intensity	Rest	Frequency
Accelerate	O,P,I	10-50 yds.	(H) 200-300 yds	Complete	Daily
Lateral	O,P,I	3-5 sets	(H) 8-10 reps	Complete	Daily

SPEED STRENGTH:

Exercise	Season	Duration/Vol.	Intensity	Rest	Frequency
Rope Jump	P	2-4 sets of 150-400 reps	(L) 17-100 contacts	1-2 min.	3 days/wk
In Place Jump	P	3-6 sets of 10-20 reps	60-120 contacts	1-2 min.	3 days/wk
Short Response/ Long Response	P	3-20 sets of 3-10 reps	40-200 contacts	2-3 min.	3 days/wk
Upper Body	P	4-10 sets of 10-20 reps	40-200 contacts	1-2 min.	3 days/wk
Plyometrics					3 days/wk

Post-Pubescent Weight Training Program
Table 2, page 3

Post-pubescent
IMPLEMENTATION:
SPEED STRENGTH:

Exercise	Season	Duration/Vol.	Intensity	Rest	Frequency
Bat Swings	O,P	9 wks. 1 oz. every 3 weeks to 34 oz. (Max.) periodic 1 oz. drops to 27 oz.			Daily
Dry Swings Batting Practice		Min. 50 cuts/bat	Stand. Hvy. Lt. Stand. Max. 100.bat	50-100	Daily
T-Work	P	1 oz. below no more than 2 oz. above weight of in-season bat			
	I	normal weight bat as much as time permits			
Medicine Ball and			2-3 kg.		Daily
Stride Length Box Combination	O,P,I	3-5 sets x 10 reps		1-2 min.	Daily

Post-pubescent
SPEED ENDURANCE

Exercise	Season	Duration/Vol.	Intensity	Rest
Sprint	O,P,I	(50-300 yds) x 1-3, 1-5 reps	(90-100%)	:45-complete (reps) 3:00-complete (sets)

O = Off-Season   L = Light
P = Pre-Season   M = Moderate
I = In-Season